BEWARE THE FALLING
AVOCADOS

Catharine Withenay

ISBN-13 978 1530660605
ISBN-10 1530660602

www.catharinewithenay.com

Disclaimer

My father once told me,
"Never let the truth get in the way of a good story."

Some facts have been twisted to make a story. Some names have
been changed. That, I'm afraid, is a writer's prerogative.

Nevertheless, this story is based upon truth, although the words
are mine alone. Even the words I have written that others have
spoken are my interpretation, not necessarily precise memories,
and so should in no way be taken as an exact representation of
others' views or opinions.

Cover design by designforwriters.com

BEWARE THE FALLING
AVOCADOS

a sequel to

IN THE SHADE OF THE
MULBERRY TREE

A Year in Zambia

ACKNOWLEDGEMENTS

'Difficult second album syndrome' hit my second book, and I am grateful to those who have kept me going through its writing and repeated edits, when otherwise I would have given up and gone to watch cricket.

For constructive criticism I have benefitted from the combined wisdom of the Poynton Writers' Guild and South Manchester Writers' Workshop, together with the editorial comments of Caroline Smailes from BubbleCow, Brett Wilson and Beverley Proctor. For proofreading my thanks go to Ann Bennett. Any and all errors that remain are entirely mine.

I am grateful to my friends in Zambia: wonderful people who have generously allowed me to fictionalise their representation in this book. I particularly thank Bernard, Eckhard, James, Jenny, Kelly, Margriet, Mike, Patrick, Peter, Precious, Rachel and Sherry. Carol, Charmaine, Julian, Tim and Tobias: you are there in spirit, even if not in print. Gwyn and Garry: I hope this book shows some of the joy we feel in your love for each other. It was a privilege to share your journey with you.

I must not forget Andrew and Rachael, and their three beautiful daughters. I couldn't have asked for better friends and loved (nearly) every minute of the holiday we shared.

My family remain my rock, to whom I am eternally grateful. My parents-in-law can verify the details of our adventurous trip to Mfuwe; my father the sign attached to the avocado tree. But above all, my thanks goes to my children and my husband. Their support, even when I write stories that embarrass them, is a tribute to their strength of character, and hopefully their senses of humour. They have given me space, time, tea and biscuits: I couldn't ask for more.

For Dad and David,
and in memory of Mum and Lois:
for their unfailing love and support.

Beware the falling avocados

Notice pinned to a tree, Lusaka

CREATURE COMFORTS

I went back for more: more of the same. I didn't expect my second year in Zambia would, once again, turn my world upside down. I knew what I anticipated: the heat, the sun, the rainy season. There would be paperwork stamped in triplicate; mindless queues to conquer bureaucratic hurdles; and wonderful people who battled on to make the country a better place, whatever the system might throw their way. People such as Sherry, our maid, nanny, housekeeper and (given those job titles) general-preserver-of-sanity, who greeted us on our return.

"Welcome home, Madame! Welcome, Bwana!"

Her broad grin mirrored my excitement. We had spent a month living out of suitcases with various friends and family in the UK: I was delighted to be back. Sherry's face lit up when she saw my children.

"And hello Matthew! And Eleanor! Look at you! My, you have grown!"

Set free from the car, Eleanor rushed headlong at Sherry, who deftly caught my cherubic 21-month-old daughter and lifted her high into the air. Eleanor beamed with joy. Not wanting to be left out, Matthew (now three-and-a-half, and pretending to be a lot more grown up) clung to Sherry's leg. She took his hand and, chattering away, led them both inside, out of the blinding sunshine. Stephen and I followed, dragging our suitcases behind.

It was home – I knew it as soon as I stepped inside. Nothing had changed. The same dreary, brown concrete floor, hand-polished by Sherry to a glorious sheen every Thursday. The dreadful pink curtains, that were supposed to be ivory but there had been a miscommunication with the seamstress. The peculiar lighting system, that only allowed the living room light to be switched off at one end if it was on at the other.

I walked through, leaving the luggage in my bedroom with its draughty louvre windows. Each of the rooms along the corridor had doors to outside with missing keys and, like most houses in Zambia, heavy iron bars as protection from burglars. At the end I reached the gloomy bathroom, still with the broken, silvered mirror, yellowing shower-head and cracked basin that had greeted me when we'd arrived in Lusaka a year earlier.

For some reason, I had wanted to come back to all this. A year earlier I had dreaded leaving the UK and, on arrival, the idiosyncrasies of the house had not improved my mood. Yet twelve months had softened my viewpoint, and I was now wishing we had more time in Zambia. Just one year left before Stephen's medical research project would be completed, and I would tolerate any of the house's problems to live here.

I was back to my life in Lusaka, and had so much to do.

I washed my hands and face, then returned to our bedroom to help Stephen unpack. He had heaved the first of our suitcases onto the bed.

"What did you put in here?" he said.

"Nothing more than you wanted. I just pack efficiently."

"Too efficiently."

"*Brownie Guide Handbook*," I declared. "If you'd read it, you would pack effectively too. Look!" The unzipped suitcase pinged open. "Nothing's moved. It all stayed in one piece and we won't have to re-iron everything."

"Hmmph," he said. "It's not as though you even do the ironing. That's Precious' job."

Our other maid, Precious, came in the afternoons to do the washing (by hand) and ironing. Sensing that Stephen's counterargument might overpower my defence, I made a tactical retreat in search of a cup of tea.

Passing through the living room I noticed Matthew and Eleanor had already pulled out a basket of toys and were playing happily. I could hear Sherry in the kitchen. She emerged carrying a tray with tea already made and laid it on the dining table, just out of my sight.

"Thank you, Sherry!"

"Madame." She bobbed her head, smiling, and withdrew to the kitchen.

"Stephen! There's tea if you want it!" I called.

A sound that I guessed to be a muffled, "Coming!" returned to me. I stepped into the dining room. It was then that I saw the flowers.

They weren't anything stunning, no fancy arrangement or vast vase of blooms. They were a handpicked bunch placed in a glass jam jar in the middle of the table. Orange, red, yellow: a blaze of colour. Flowers picked from our garden, some of them beginning to wilt.

If they had been arranged by the finest florist in fashionable London they would have had less impact. Sherry must have put them there earlier, with no prompting or encouragement: a simple gesture to welcome us home. To me they were worth a million dollars.

Biting my lip to hold back tears, I poured the tea, wondering why I deserved such generosity. Then I sat and stared at the flowers, warmed more by love than by the mug of tea.

࿐

As the light poured out from the open fridge, I could have sworn I saw something scuttle away underneath. I stared at the spot on the floor where I thought it had been, waiting for it to reappear. Nothing. Perhaps I'd imagined it. I could hear nothing but the silent hum of the fridge and the distant croaking of frogs. Three o'clock in the morning was too early for the cockerels in Kalingalinga, or the peacocks in the neighbouring road.

I took out the orange juice and placed it to one side. Stephen, who had Type 1 Diabetes, was hypoglycaemic and needed the sugary drink. There was an irony in this nocturnal visit to the fridge. Forget the need for beds, tables and chairs: when we had arrived the previous year the fridge had been the most important item of furniture missing from the house. A fridge allowed me to keep milk cool and fresh, and to freeze mushed up food in ice-cubes as I weaned my baby daughter. In my rush to acquire one, it had never crossed my mind that the fridge was also necessary to store Stephen's insulin, so low down was he on my list of concerns. My mind had been focused on protecting my children. I was so furious with my husband for dragging us to Africa that his needs had come a very poor second.

The refrigerator had been our first Zambian acquisition and, for me, the first sign that there could be normality in this strange land. Not only could I buy a fridge in the shops, just like in the UK, but I had a choice of models, size and design. Better still, it had been delivered the next day, at the time they specified – a quality of service that had not always been replicated on every occasion since, mind you.

Now, in the middle of our first night back in Lusaka, it wasn't the children but Stephen I was worrying about. I had a hierarchy of options when Stephen was hypoglycaemic: Lucozade, orange juice, piece of chocolate. I rarely had to resort to giving him the last one, though it often calmed my nerves after a bad attack. If we were out, then stopping for a very sugary coffee usually did the trick. The hypos didn't happen often, but I did resent their disturbance in the middle of the night and I was cursing my foolishness at not replenishing the stock of Lucozade. Still, the orange would have to do.

I stared at the chocolate on the fridge shelf, tempting me as it had done all day. *No! I have the juice. I'll remain strong.* I shut the fridge door and lost all light. The fridge shuddered as its systems switched off then, ominously, I heard a scratching noise from behind.

In my haste to flick on the main light switch I knocked the carton, spilling sticky juice all over the kitchen surface. I swore and reached for a cloth. It was underneath the plate I'd left in the sink after a cheeky late-night slice of toast. A procession of ants was marching across the draining board and straight to the remaining crumbs. If it hadn't been the middle of the night I might have enjoyed watching them for a while, as they picked up bits of toast half their bodyweight and carried them back home. Instead I splashed water into the washing-up bowl, killing a few of God's creatures, and retrieved the cloth.

Turning back I thought I heard the scratching again. I stared intently under the fridge. Nothing emerged. No sound. I was probably safe.

Involuntarily, I shivered. Night-time was the worst. All the creatures seemed to be out and none of them wanted you to see them, except the moths that now were flapping around the bare light bulb overhead. It had only been a couple of minutes and already there were three dancing for their lives.

Wiping up the juice I thought back to when we had been in the UK a few weeks earlier. Travelling from my father's to my parents-in-law's Stephen had turned greyer and greyer, until I'd had to pull over to allow him to be sick. Ever the sympathetic nurse, I wasn't too pleased that I wouldn't be able to share the burden of driving the comparatively long journey, and even less pleased at the prospect of him throwing up all over the hire car. We eventually got to Norwich where he spent a feverish night with frequent visits to the bathroom.

At the time it had only been a few days since leaving Zambia, so I had my emergency radar on full alert. The symptoms were consistent with malaria and none of the rest of us felt ill. I knew he had to get checked out. Therein lay the battle: my husband was a doctor, so didn't do hospitals except to work in them. "But it's the dry season. There isn't malaria in Lusaka," he had complained. I had ignored his remarks and driven him to A&E, leaving the children to have some quality time with Grannie and Grampa.

Norwich isn't a hotbed for malaria. The hospital was newly built and only recently opened, so the facilities were fantastic. The nurse had taken an armful of blood and, while it was sent for testing in the laboratory, the medical care had gone into overdrive and checked him out for anything else that might be a problem. He was sent for a chest X-ray and had an ECG, so we were confident that his heart and lungs worked satisfactorily. His blood sugars were taken regularly which, given his diabetes, was to be expected. Neither of us was surprised that they were all over the place (a common result of fighting infections).

After four hours the malaria blood tests had finally come back negative. By that time he was feeling better and we'd already self-diagnosed a virus, to be treated with patience and lots of fluids. He retreated to his parents' house to rest.

Back in Lusaka, I finished mopping up the juice. It was winter, a time of minimal threat of malaria. It was also too late at night (or early in the morning) for the crepuscular malarial mosquitoes to be a concern. My trek to the kitchen had merely been threatened by mice, moths and ants. *Honestly girl,* I thought, *in a country where lions and leopards roam wild, these are hardly the most dangerous of predators.*

I took a glass from the cupboard and filled it with juice, returned the carton to the fridge, switched off the kitchen light and began to head back to the bedroom.

Then I had second thoughts. I opened the fridge again. *It was forward thinking, surely, to take the chocolate too... just in case...?*

NO PLACE LIKE HOME

I loved the café.

In the midst of the madness of a shopping mall, and following the stress of trying to squeeze a family of four's shop onto one trolley, the cafe was a place of refuge. Every time I walked in, my stress levels dropped a measurable amount. At the first opportunity on our return I escaped both work and the children to meet up with friends for a coffee.

It was a cavernous venue, the more so because of the ceiling being open to the pipework for the air-conditioning and wiring. When it first opened this gave the café an incomplete character, but as time went by the empty walls were filled with paintings, and the rafters became hidden by the art of local artists, clipped on with clothes pegs. Gradually the room was filled with the creative work of many locals – not just pictures, but carvings, flags, metalwork, jewellery, bags. The terracotta-coloured paint, prevalent throughout Zambia, was swiftly hidden.

The owners clearly knew their market. The expat housewife, with children round her feet, was instantly assuaged. (Sometimes it was a househusband, but that was a lot less common.) The long counter displayed a wide range of cakes and pastries (take-away or eat in), and towards the back a couple of rugs and some baskets of toys allowed their young children to be entertained. The big tub of Lego was enough to keep most children happy for half an hour; cars and dolls were a bonus. At weekends it was packed with families coming for a cooked breakfast, or waffles with maple syrup, but mornings midweek were more commonly harassed mothers, instantly appeased by a coffee and cake.

It had only taken a week for the excitement of returning to Lusaka to drain away. The resumption of work brought back all the suppressed frustrations with African life: Stephen cursed the hospital's inefficiencies; I cursed colleagues who didn't request petty cash in time; we both despaired at poor time-keeping. Our commute to work was not held up by traffic jams but by street traders at the traffic lights, selling cheap imported plastic toys or boxes of fruit (deceitfully hiding empty spaces beneath the cardboard flap). I was back to judging which vehicles were the most unroadworthy: taxis held together with duck-tape, lorries that had lost all suspension and wheel alignment or minibuses that thought they owned the road.

The 'summer holiday' (which I couldn't help calling the long break, even in a southern-hemisphere winter) had sent expats like us back to our home countries and I couldn't wait to hear all my friends' news. Jenny, a quietly spoken South African, was wisdom personified and a friend I naturally turned to when confused. Margriet's ebullience was a delightful contrast: somehow she always made me smile. She had lived in Africa for many years, gradually working her way further south, and we'd been on holiday with her, her husband Eckhard and their children the previous Easter. Her English was excellent, but all the years in Africa hadn't diminished her Dutch accent. We had fallen into a Friday routine of meeting for a chat after we'd left our children at school and finished the supermarket shop. For me it was a therapy session.

"Wow! That's a mountain of food!" exclaimed Jenny on seeing my overburdened trolley.

"We have friends arriving from the UK so I thought I'd better stock up," I said. As I gazed on the pile of shopping I wondered if it was excessive. My friend's three children were under the age of five, so couldn't possibly eat that much... *could they?*

"Never mind," said Margriet, leaning over to greet me with a European kiss on the cheeks. "It is good to see you, and to be prepared, no?"

"Hey, yes Margriet, and if there's any left over we can go round and help finish it off!" said Jenny. Already laughing together, it was as if we'd never been apart.

I gave them a wry smile. "You'd be most welcome, but my suspicion is that it will all go without any difficulty."

"Ah yes," said Margriet, "nothing lasts long in our house any more. My three don't seem to stop eating."

"Not like children in the UK though, I'm sure. I was astonished how fat they all looked! I found myself staring at a poor girl at the shopping mall, perhaps eight years old, sucking a lolly. Given how podgy she was I couldn't help but think, 'You shouldn't be having sweets!'"

"You are too used to the poverty here," said

Margriet.

I thought of the skinny street beggars I saw every day. So many in Zambia would crave food we threw away in the UK.

"A husband who works with malnourished kids and I've become judgemental about overconsumption," I mused. The waitress materialised beside us, poised for our order. "Still, it's not going to stop me getting a croissant now." I compounded my hypocrisy by ordering a hot chocolate to go with it.

Settling back on the sofa, Jenny asked if I had found it strange going back to the UK.

"In what way?"

"Well, being home, and the different culture and ways of doing things."

"Oh yes!" I said, thinking back to our visit. "The first morning I went to buy a newspaper and stood there in the corner shop literally staring at the coins in my hand, wondering what was what, and how many I needed. Bizarre, given I've lived with those coins for over thirty years."

"A year of just notes and it's strange to have that weight in your purse."

"Exactly! For days I felt I was carrying around a dead weight in my bag and I would check to see if I'd picked up something by accident. It was a real culture shock to return to the British way of life."

"At least you drive on the same side of the road," said Margriet. "Every time I get confused trying to find the gear stick."

"Fair point, although the wipers and indicators were on the other side of the steering wheel on all the cars I drove, so I spent a lot of time cleaning my windscreen when I wanted to turn right!"

My demonstration of how the wipers had worked nearly sent our drinks flying, as the waitress appeared from behind me with our order. "Sorry!" I said. "Here, let me take them from your tray."

I gave Jenny her drink, and then passed Margriet her coffee as she continued speaking. "But it is also good, yes, to be back home? Me, I like the cheese – some mature Gouda. Holland is the only place to really get this."

I nearly melted into the chair as I remembered the cheese aisle. "Cheese! Oh, how wonderful it was to have choice! Creamy, crumbly, blue… it was magnificent. And prawn cocktail flavoured crisps! I hadn't realised I'd missed them until I stopped dead in my tracks in the supermarket and exclaimed, 'Crisps!' in far too loud a voice."

"You must have been a sight!" said Margriet, laughing.

"I know! I was pathetic! It took me ages to get used to things like that again, simple luxuries, like taking water from the tap."

"You have water in taps here," Jenny said, sipping her coffee.

"Yes, but not drinking water. Here we have to filter everything, and I've clearly got used to that intermediary step. Every time I went for a glass of water I thought twice before turning the tap on. Was it safe? Could I trust it?"

"It's astonishing what you get used to," said Jenny.

"Anyway, how about you? What's happened? What did I miss when I was gone?"

I grabbed the chance to take a slurp of my hot chocolate, and sat back to listen. I couldn't keep a smile from my face. This was what I had missed, so much of what I had come to love about living in Zambia: a feeling that time didn't matter. The UK's twenty-four-hour culture seemed to eat away at this type of relaxation, a constant consumerism and demand for services that didn't allow space. In turn this meant people were under pressure to be available at all times, so they had to work longer hours, or more flexibly. Is that what wealth does to a nation? It wasn't as if we didn't have things to do in Lusaka; nevertheless I carved out this Friday morning space to recharge batteries and put all the troubles of the week in perspective.

In Africa there was always time. Sometimes too much time (I thought of Stephen's frustrations with the two-hour lunch breaks some colleagues took at work), but always enough time. There was never stress to be punctual at parties, or any social event, and yet it was rare for anything to be delayed. *How on earth did that work?* I wondered. Time: the most precious of commodities, that we can never get back, but which we can't help spending.

"I hear that there is a new internet supplier in town," I caught Margriet saying. "They're advertising broadband. Eckhard's looking into it for work."

"Wow, that would be great!" I said, thinking of the achingly slow connection speed we achieved on the phone line. One of the first pieces of advice I'd been given during the last rainy season was to unplug the phone, due to the risk of a power surge in the storms, but even more so to protect the internet connection. The last thing we wanted was to destroy the computer.

"Their claims are impressive. I'll pass on the information, if you're interested, and let you know how Eckhard gets on."

"Thanks! It's astonishing how technology changes," I said. "The car we hired only had a CD player with its radio – no tapes. I thought I'd been so clever, having borrowed some cassettes so I could play storybooks and songs to the children as we drove around. But I was thwarted by technology."

"Oh no! Did Matthew and Eleanor mind?"

"Nah, we just sang loudly instead!"

"I can well imagine," said Jenny wryly.

"Now, now! We're not that bad!" I said in mock horror. "Though I'd give you that if you were referring to Stephen, of course."

"Aren't his parents visiting soon?"

"Yes, in a couple of weeks. Friends leave, family arrive."

"Including Gwyn?" said Margriet.

"Yes. We're all really excited about that." Stephen's sister had taken up a teaching post at the international primary school attached to the pre-school Matthew attended. Her visit was a lot more long term than her parents. "The flat across the way from ours will be free from the end of the month, so she'll stay with us for a few weeks first. She'll have to get some furniture, if nothing else!"

"And that will take a while to find, and make."

"I know."

"Remind me, how long's her contract?" Jenny asked.

"Two years," I replied.

"And you? How much longer does Stephen have here?"

"Just the year," I said with a smile.

"Ach, that is too soon," interjected Margriet with a broad grin. "We have another two years."

"Yes, Catharine, you should stay longer!" Jenny joked, and I laughed only to be brought up short by Margriet.

"No, no, Jenny's right," she said. "You must tell Stephen that a year is not long enough. OK?"

Margriet's sparkling eyes were a contrast to her strict tone of voice. Still, there was no messing with her. I felt truly told what I should be doing.

I licked my finger and picked up the final tantalising crumbs of croissant. An hour had passed without a gap in conversation. My hot chocolate had been drawn out for as long as possible. It was time to leave.

But now a little voice was screaming in my ear: *we should stay here. We should put down roots, settle the family and educate our children. We are fit and healthy: we should enjoy this marvellous country while we can.*

How on earth would we do that?

JUST A LITTLE LONGER

The house creaked with the night-time silence. Draughts blew in through gaps that were designed to keep the building cool during the oppressive heat of October. But it was August, and the winds slipped through the crack beneath the front door, gusting dust around a house that had not retained heat from the daylight hours. My children were fast asleep and Stephen was working at the computer in the back room. I wandered round the living room performing my nightly duty of picking up toys. For once, I was grateful for the banality of the chore, my mind whirling.

"You should stay longer," my friends had said.

Could we? Could that really be possible?

There were so many things to think through. Firstly, there was the practicality of staying. I tossed some soft toys into a woven basket and looked around. I was settled. I'd furnished the living room with a sofa and chair, and we had bespoke furniture fitted neatly into the spaces. A separate bedroom for Eleanor would be nice, but she and Matthew were hardly of an age for that to matter: I was planning for them as teenagers way before their time. *One more year would keep me in line with Margriet. Surely we could squeeze another year in, somehow? It would be lovely to put off moving house and – worse still – country.*

Spotting Baby James wedged under the sofa I bent down to pick him up. I brushed dust off the doll and smiled at the memories he brought back. James had had his name embroidered on the bib when purchased, though that had long since been lost. He had been Matthew's baby when Eleanor was born: his baby to play with while I dealt with a newborn. The theory was that it would prevent the then two-year-old Matthew feeling left out by his sister's arrival. In reality, he was never very bothered by the new intrusion in his life. I settled James into the basket with the other toys.

Would it matter staying longer? The kids would love it. Eleanor would continue to delight everyone by running around, her sunny temperament matching the Zambian weather. Matthew…

I froze mid-task. Next year he would be due to start primary school. *How did that happen? How did my baby grow to be of an age for school, for proper education? It would become serious; I wouldn't be able to take him out of class on a whim for an adventure.*

What would happen if he didn't take his place in the state system back home? Then again, what quality did the state system in central London offer? Here he would start his formal education in a private school, in a small class of about twenty. It could be better for him.

Then I wondered if we could afford it. I abandoned the toys and rushed to the other side of the room to rummage through some paperwork. I knew I'd seen Matthew's school prospectus when I was sorting out bills earlier. My fears were confirmed. Reception class more than doubled the fees we paid for pre-school. *How would we fund that?*

I sighed and put the papers away. Financially it was a daft idea to stay on. We couldn't live off air and my salary was nothing to write home about. Stephen's funding would run out next year and that was that. He was required to spend two years in the UK to complete his registrar training and then he could apply for consultant posts. That was his timescale, and thus ours.

Though a little devil then whispered in my ear: *You could stay while he went back home. He'd write his PhD up much more quickly without the distractions of children.*

"Don't be ridiculous!"

Did I say that out loud? I looked around the empty room to see if anyone had heard me. There was no sound other than the steady tap-tap-tap from Stephen typing in the other room. If I did speak, he certainly wasn't disturbed by my voice.

I slumped onto the sofa. *Am I going mad? Me? Stay here? Without him?*

I began to think it through. We were settled here. I had support – friends and, with the imminent arrival of Gwyn, family – and the services of Sherry and Precious. Back in London? I'd be on my own (I'd had plenty of experience of Stephen's working hours, combined with him being on-call overnight two or three times a week) and unable to afford the childcare support that our maids offered. I rationalised that, for about the same amount of money, I might get six hours of a cleaner's time per month in London. That hardly compared to the six days a week I got at present.

No, the sensible thing would be for me to stay here and Stephen to go back to the UK. He could complete his studies and then, when he'd qualified as a consultant, we could join him for his permanent job. *Or he could apply for more funding to come back here.*

I smiled, because I knew that was what Stephen would want most of all. He was in his element in Lusaka, working with the malnourished children. I sat quietly for a moment, listening for the tapping of the keyboard and the occasional shuffling of papers. Despite all the frustrations he voiced, his work here was never a chore. He would be back at the drop of a hat.

I threw back my head and ran my hands through my hair. *Madness! Madness! Madness! Why are you even considering this?* I thought. *You have a year left. Concentrate on filling it to the full. Think of all the things you'd like to do.*

I stared around the room, still littered with toys. There were many things I wanted to do but tidying up was not one of them. For me, one of the perks of living in Zambia was having Sherry and Precious to clean the house. Some women didn't like having staff in their homes doing all the work, but I had succumbed easily. I sighed. Tomorrow the toys would all be thrown around again. I dragged myself off the sofa to return to deal with the mess and, as some form of motivation, decided to think of one more place I'd like to visit in Zambia with each toy tidied away.

"South Luangwa," I said, putting the drum in the basket. That was a bit of a cheat, because we were taking Stephen's parents there in a few weeks' time. The Victoria Falls got a similar put down.

"Lake Bangweulu." Timmy the soldier went back in his barracks. I checked the space rocket jigsaw for lost pieces.

"Lake Tanganika."

"Kafue National Park." *Elephants. Please let me see more elephants. And lions. And leopards too. In fact, the whole 'Big Five' please.*

"The chimps?" I wasn't so sure about them. Animals held in captivity were nowhere near as enticing as animals in the wild.

"The Kumboka ceremony."

There wouldn't be enough time. All those places to visit, within one year? Even if we took a six-week final road-trip we'd be lucky to squeeze them all in.

I stepped backwards onto a sticklebrick. "Aargh!" I yelled, hopping round in a circle to shake off the pain. When I stopped it struck me that *that* hadn't attracted Stephen's attention either. *So engrossed in his research he's oblivious to my pain and anxiety*, I thought begrudgingly.

Throwing the last of the offending toys into baskets and stacking the books on the shelves, I decided I'd make him a hot chocolate and encourage him to stop for the night. With a barely perceptible limp I carried the mugs through to the spare room.

"Stephen?" I called to his back. "Stephen?" I repeated, much louder and sharper.

He pulled his headphones from his ears and turned around. "You OK?"

He hadn't heard a word I'd said. I spoke more softly. "Yes, I'm fine. Are you nearly finished?"

"Just got to enter a few more patients' data," he said, indicating a pile of files.

The to-do pile didn't look much smaller than the one he'd spent two hours working through. I gave him his drink and turned to go, then thought better of it. It was never just going to be my decision, and I had to share some of my turbulent thoughts with my best friend.

"Have you got a moment to talk? There's something we need to discuss."

THE PROFESSOR SAID TO THE BISHOP...

"Everyone ready?"

A general grunting that I took to be 'yes' came from the back of The Professor. I got a thumbs-up from our friends in The Bishop so, glad to finally be on our way, I locked the front door and sank into the driving seat. The early morning, plus the stress of packing four adults and five children into our two cars, ready for a five hundred kilometre journey to see the Victoria Falls, had worn me out.

"I'll be glad when we get there," I said to Stephen. "Is Eleanor going to be OK?"

I glanced anxiously in the rear-view mirror. She was dozing in her car seat, now covered by an old towel.

"She'll be fine. She hasn't been sick again and I

suspect after a good sleep she'll be right as rain," Stephen said.

"It's a long journey," I warned him. "Let's hope she sleeps the whole way."

I drove carefully through the city centre, checking in my mirror not only to ascertain Eleanor's status (asleep) but also to ensure our friends were following. Weaving in and out of traffic down Independence and around Kamwata made this a challenge.

"Still there?" Stephen asked as we queued over the bridge.

"Yep, though a few cars back. I hope they're all right: I found all this quite daunting when we first arrived."

In a light bulb moment, Stephen reached into the bag at his feet. "We've got just the thing!" he said, pulling out a walkie-talkie.

"That?" I queried. We'd been given a pair as a gift some time ago, before we left the UK. I'd always thought them pointless.

"It's perfect," he said. "We won't get any mobile connectivity once we're out of the city. I've finally found a use for them. Besides, I think it might be entertaining."

There was a buzz and a crackle from the walkie-talkie. He turned the device over in his hands, checking the battery compartment and fiddling with the buttons. I tried to ignore him and concentrate on my driving as I dodged vehicles on the Kafue Road.

"How do these things work?" he asked.

"How on earth am I supposed to know?" I snapped back, narrowly avoiding two men who had chosen that moment to push their laden wheelbarrow across the six lanes of traffic. Their presence had only become obvious when the minibus in front of me careered across two of the lanes in order to pick up passengers. Sucking air in through my teeth, I was not interested in the gadgetry that Stephen was holding.

"Aha!" he said with a glow of triumph. He raised the walkie-talkie to his mouth and spoke.

"Blue one to Red one – over."

"Blue one to Red one? What on earth are you playing at?" I asked.

"It's the way they do it, isn't it? Messaging over the airwaves?"

Our friends evidently understood more quickly than me, as the reply came swiftly:

"Red one to Blue one – over."

"It works! It works!" Stephen said excitedly. *"Everything OK with you? Over."*

"Yes, fine here. How much further have we to go? Over."

"You sound like my children! We haven't left Lusaka yet. Livingstone's miles away. Over."

"Shame." There was a pause.

"Are we supposed to talk now?" I asked. "He hasn't said, 'Over' yet."

"Sshh!" Stephen hissed, as a further response came.

"Is Eleanor all right? Over."

"So far. I think she's sleeping off her upset stomach. Over."

"Poor girl. At least her timing was good: to throw up before we left, rather than en route. Over."

"Yeah, though I'd still have preferred not to have had to clean it up. Over."

"Too true. We'll leave you in peace to let her snooze. Over."

"Thank you! Over and out."

Stephen put aside the walkie-talkie and twisted in his seat to look at our daughter.

"OK?" I asked.

"Yes," he said, settling back to face the front. "As I said: sleeping it off."

I smiled. "Let's hope that's the last of it, that she just ate something at breakfast that disagreed with her," I said. "Many miles to go and the last thing we need is more vomit."

Stephen couldn't help fidgeting, turning the walkie-talkie in his hands. He lifted it to his mouth. I raised an eyebrow.

"I thought I'd give them a tour guide," he said, "as we go through the day."

I stared at the road ahead of me. *Oh heck*, I thought.

The first point of interest to Stephen was at Chilanga.

"Blue one to Red one – over."

"Red one to Blue one – over."

"Look out for the concrete elephants on your left."

"Oh yes!"

"And lions on your right. Possibly."

"Concrete lions?"

"No, real ones, in the zoo. Their caging was just by the road there. We're past it now, and I didn't spot them, sorry. Over and out."

Munda Wanga was a neat little zoo, set to the side of the Botanical Gardens. Technically it was now known as an Environmental Park, but the old name stuck. Most of the animals were endemic to Zambia, housed at the zoo in order to protect them, some from poachers or illegal animal traders, others had been orphaned. The stark exception was the tiger, that lay on a wooden platform, shaded by a large tree, looking as if he'd rather be home in Asia: or, indeed, anywhere but there.

While the zoo was worth a wander round, the Botanical Gardens were the real draw. I was no botanist, but I appreciated the planting and the mature trees that shaded the grounds. Here we could bring the children to run around and explore in relative safety, and enjoy a picnic in the shade of a mululu tree.

As we drove past the entrance I thought that I should take my friends there when we got back from our trip to the Victoria Falls.

A little further on and there was buzz and crackle from our handset before they spoke.

"Red one to Blue one – over."

"Blue one to Red one – over."

"Giraffes?" The astonishment in her voice made it squeak over the airwaves.

"Carvings of all sizes."

"Yeah, all sizes, but many at six foot. What do you do with them?"

"Absolutely no idea. Stand them in your living room and remember Africa, I guess. I've seen queues at the airport with people holding wooden giraffes taller than themselves."

"How do they get them onto the aircraft without breaking them?"

"Haven't a clue!"

There was a pause, followed by a further exclamation from our friends.

"There's loads! Yet another stall just there. Can they possibly sell enough to make a living?"

"Hard to imagine, isn't it?"

"Particularly as we're flying past at… what, a hundred kilometres per hour."

"I know! But they're just along this bit of road. Then it's something else. Bananas, I think. Over and out."

We surmounted a hill and the vast valley of the Kafue flats came into view, spreading lazily across the landscape. "You should warn them about the checkpoint," I said to Stephen. He resumed his conversation.

"This is the Kafue river – the flats, where it spreads out before its final passage to the Zambezi. After the bridge there's a police checkpoint where we'll have to stop."

"OK. Anything we should be aware of?"

"Never been questioned before. Always a first time though…"

"Thanks! Makes me feel a lot more confident."

"My pleasure!"

"I love the sign! 'The police do not take bribes.' Says a lot about expectations! Over and out."

To date we had never had any real grief at a police checkpoint, not even the previous New Year when it was only on our way home from holiday that I'd remembered I hadn't brought the new tax disk to display on the windscreen. It had made for an anxious encounter, but they'd kindly waved us through.

My suspicion was that this checkpoint was more to investigate the overloaded lorries than to worry about tourist traffic. The opposite side of the road had melted and moulded like lumpy custard. The heavy juggernauts all pulling to a standstill during the heat of the day caused the road to buckle and I wondered how, or if, the Zambian government would get round to repairing it.

"Thank you, sir," I said in polite deference to the white-gloved policeman as he waved me through. I drove off slowly, holding The Bishop in the rear-view mirror. It was an agonising wait as the policeman walked slowly round to my friend at the driver's side (why wasn't the police hut in the middle of the road?) and asked his questions, stuck his head in The Bishop to check its occupants, stood back to consider his verdict and then, begrudgingly, waved them on.

I let out my breath, but Stephen was already back on the walkie-talkie.

"Phew! Glad that's over. Over."

I looked at Stephen. Really?

"Ha ha – yes, all was OK. Over."

"Nothing much to excite you in Kafue town, I'm afraid. Our next point of interest is the right turn ahead, by the big sugar sign. Then, finally, we'll be on the road to Livingstone. Over."

"Roger. Over and out."

The road south to Livingstone took a scenic route

through the Munali Pass before reaching the sugar capital of Mazabuka. The journey through the range of hills was stunning although, as with all Zambian roads that involve a small incline, there was always the risk of coming across a broken-down bus or lorry. It felt safer if this happened on your side of the road, as all that was required was to slow down (or stop, even) then take extreme caution in overtaking. If the breakdown was on the opposite side of the road, then you were at the mercy of the oncoming drivers. Lorry drivers in a hurry didn't seem very concerned about the etiquette, or safety, of pulling out into oncoming traffic.

Stephen updated me from the guidebook. Apparently the name 'munali' meant 'redhead' in the local language and was a physical attribute of David Livingstone. It was from the top of one of these hills that he first saw the Kafue river. I don't know what time of year that would have been, but spread out over the flats it must have been an awesome sight. How did they get across? They didn't have the advantage of the bridge we'd just crossed. There was a roadside monument to Livingstone's discovery, in a patronising colonial way, given it had existed for years and was no 'discovery' to the locals. Stephen pointed it out as we whizzed past.

"It is so beautiful here," I said, sneaking glimpses either side as I drove. "They could make so much more of the place by attracting tourists and celebrating Livingstone's presence here."

"Yeah, but tourists might destroy it," Stephen said. "More buses, more litter, more people ambling across the busy road. It could be a disaster."

"Fair point. Let's keep it a secret for ourselves."

"We're not stopping now, anyway," he said. "Onwards, onwards – ever onwards!" he declared as if he were directing the Salvation Army. "Livingstone's town is our destination, not his lookout tower."

"Though he did stand on an island mid-stream when he first saw the Victoria Falls," I pointed out. "A unique and precarious lookout tower."

"Maybe I should try walking over the top of the Falls to Livingstone Island," he mused.

"You will not!" I said. "I'm not so bothered about you, but I don't want you giving Matthew ideas. I'm expecting a lot of water at this time of year – certainly more than when we visited last December."

We drove on through the bustling town of Mazabuka and out into the fairly flat countryside between there and Livingstone. The early European settlers had learnt from the Romans and built wide, straight roads with little in the way of twists and turns. Stephen's running commentary ground to a halt. The occasional settlement would curve us round some bends, and we chopped and changed which side of the line of rail we paralleled. Monze provided a toilet stop and a short break for our late lunch; otherwise we were set for an unremarkable journey.

"Nobody ate much," I commented to Stephen.

"It's a long day," he said. "Three hours' driving already; at least another four to go. Why is travel like this so exhausting when really we are doing nothing?"

"I don't know. Eleanor's perked up a bit, though. In fact, she possibly ate more than Matthew."

To prove a point, she voiced some of her happiness with a series of gurgles and ill-formed words, dipping in and out of her newly composed song. Matthew gave her a disdainful look then returned to reading his book.

Walkie-talkie in hand, Stephen paused before speaking. "Are we Red or Blue?" he asked me.

I laughed. "Blue. At least, so far. Much of it is a purple mush."

"Oh, ha ha," he said, then into the speaker: *"Blue one*

to Red one – over."

"Red one to Blue one – over."

"Nearly forgot what colour we were. Could we avoid confusion and change to being The Professor and The Bishop?"

"Sounds like the start of a dodgy joke! Who's the Bishop?"

"Actually you are. We named the cars after the people we bought them from. The Pajero you're driving used to belong to a bishop and our Starlet was a professor's."

"So we're high up and can lord it over you?"

I groaned.

"Yes, but we're cleverer," Stephen responded quickly.

"I know. I was at school with your wife."

That made me give a wry smile. Stephen wasn't going to allow me to get big-headed though.

"But you'll be closer to God."

"Might need that on roads like these," came the response, uncannily coinciding with a swerve to avoid a pothole. There was never a dull moment when travelling in Zambia. *"Over and out."*

After a little while, Stephen said, ominously, "I've been thinking."

"Oh yeah?"

"About your suggestion. About staying longer."

I gulped and kept stony quiet.

"I see the logic in your thinking. It might work."

"It's not as financially bonkers as it sounds at first," I said. "I've done a spreadsheet."

Stephen smiled. "I can't take the accountant out of you, can I?"

"Nope!"

I grinned. He was silent and serious again. "Would you manage – I mean, really manage – on your own?"

Tempting though it was, I didn't belittle his concern with a flippant reply. In many ways it hinged on this: could I cope?

"I suppose I won't know until I try," was my

measured response. "But, if it truly is awful, I'll come home. We'll always find the money for that."

A thoughtful silence fell.

"Mum and Dad won't be impressed by us keeping their grandchildren away from them," he said almost absent-mindedly.

"Hey! They've got another one now, safely in the UK. They'll cope!"

But it was true, and given their imminent visit I realised we'd have to mention it to them. After all my complaints about coming to Zambia in the first place, it was going to be strange to let them know I wanted to stay longer than originally planned.

"I'll look into what I can do, work-wise," Stephen said. "The experiment is taking longer than anticipated to get the right cohort, so I've been advised to apply for an extra six months' funding. Let's see where we get to with that first."

"OK," I agreed, and we settled back to enjoy the view, each mulling over the permutations of staying or moving. There were many miles ahead to Livingstone and virtually nothing of note. Miles and miles of uninteresting road and flat scrubland, dotted with termite mounds.

In retrospect, I'd have settled for the boredom of a repetitive landscape and a swift journey to our destination. Instead there was a series of interruptions.

"Bishop to the Professor – over."

"Professor to the Bishop – over."

"Need to stop. Emergency. Over."

"Roger. Shady tree ahead. Over and out."

A short while after this first unexpected stop Stephen checked in on our friends in The Bishop.

"Everything all right back there? Over."

"Yes. We stopped just in time. She's holding the bowl now, but seems a lot perkier. Thank you. Over."

"No worries! Let's hope that's the last of it. Over."

"Great! I just don't want anyone to be sick over..." my friend quipped. We laughed.

"We don't want it to be either over or out," Stephen replied, flicking off the walkie-talkie.

"How much further do we have to go?" I asked him. He checked the map at the front of the guidebook.

"Still to go through Choma, then Kaloma, then the long stretch down to Livingstone," he said.

"That last bit's where the road needs resurfacing, isn't it?"

"Yeah. Maybe they'll have started working on it?"

I gave Stephen a look. "We both know that's improbable. I haven't heard of any foreign governments offering to prop up Zambia's tourist trade in that manner. Sensible people," I reflected, "would fly."

"Next time, next time..."

"I need a wee!" screamed Matthew from the back.

"Can you wait?" I asked.

"No! I need it now!"

I cursed. We'd only just got going again.

"I really, really need a wee!" he wailed.

"OK! OK!"

Stephen took up the walkie-talkie again.

"The Professor to The Bishop."

"Bishop reading you loud and clear."

"Toilet stop required. Pulling over at next tree."

"Roger."

It turned out that Matthew's sudden stop was fortuitous timing. Almost as soon as we stopped, their second daughter emptied her stomach into the bushes.

"Two down, one to go?" I asked them.

"Oh! Don't think like that! We must be done now."

"I hope so!" I glanced anxiously at Matthew. *Did he really just need a wee, or was his stomach also churning?* I crossed my fingers and resumed driving.

Of course, not much further on, we had need to stop again.

"Professor to The Bishop."

"Bless you, my child."

"Matthew says he's not feeling well. We'll pull over soon."

"OK. Over and out."

A few minutes later I stood in the shade of a tree, watching while yet another of my friend's children threw up. Stephen had dealt with Matthew, rinsed out the bowls we'd brought and come to stand beside me.

"You wouldn't think there could be any more to come out, would you?" I said.

"With children, there always seems to be more to come out. And usually over me."

I kissed him on the cheek. "Thanks for dealing with that. If it's any consolation, Eleanor's nappy wasn't much fun either."

"At least she's been fine the whole journey, so we must be about done."

"We'd better be – it really reeks in the car."

"Not far to go now."

I looked up at the sky. "Good job! The sun will be gone before long."

"We've a couple of hours," my optimistic husband said.

But when I got back in the car I remembered we still had the stretch from Kaloma to do: that could take forever.

After passing through the nondescript town, our friends evidently had the same thought.

"Bishop to The Professor."

"Professor reading you."

"What happened to the road?"

"It's just in need of a little upgrading."

"Upgrading? It's a slalom course to avoid all the holes."

"Yeah, it's not great... but they are working on it. See 'roadworks ahead'."

"There was nobody there."

"True enough, but the thought was there. And the cones."

"Not sure what this is doing for the upset stomachs."

"Valid point. I'll try to get Catharine to slow down a little."

"I can't believe the way she drives! She wasn't like this when we were at school!"

"She's training as a rally cross driver in her spare time."

"Stephen!" I exclaimed. "You can't say that!"

Then I wondered if it was actually a compliment. The next hour was spent weaving and winding my way around various holes in the tarmac, and overtaking the odd trundling van carrying its precious load of mealie meal, or pigs, or firewood. The sun was setting and, as was usual with all our long-distance journeys, we were late.

The first rule for safe driving in Zambia was not to drive in the dark. Despite the law, many vehicles didn't have working lights, which combined with the precarious state of their chassis and loads, did not bode well. There were additional fears if our car were to break down, or if we met unscrupulous carjackers. We always planned to arrive at our destination at around 16 hours, to give us time to settle in before sunset. Somehow, this never materialised.

To my right I watched the sky turn orange, with a purple haze across a couple of random clouds that formed an arrow shape. It was as if they were showing us the way to Livingstone.

I saw movement on the road ahead. There was a final flurry on the walkie-talkies.

"The Professor to The Bishop."

"Mrs Bishop here. Crikey! I've turned into an episode of Neighbours!"

"Are you OK?"

"Yes, fine. I'll be glad when we stop though. The girls are snoozing."

"Same here. There's a police block ahead so you'll need your travel documents to hand."

"Does that mean we're here? We've reached Livingstone?"

I could hear some whooping in the background. We were all relieved to finally be arriving.

"Pretty much. The town's just around the corner: a drive down a street of sleeping policemen."

"Past one policeman and over several others, eh?"

"Yep! But at least the road improves now. Over and out."

Drawing into the hotel car park, I slumped back in my seat. We'd made it. The sun had said goodbye for the night but we were safely at the hotel. Stephen checked us in but we declined the reception's kind offers of food, apart from a few slices of plain toast. We'd seen enough food, in both directions, for one day. We parted from our friends, promising to meet them at breakfast in the morning.

Stephen read a bedtime story to the children while I sloshed a pile of clothes and towels around in the bath. I pitied the maid who'd clean up the debris in the morning. It was a shame that shutting the en suite door didn't eliminate the all-pervasive smell of vomit.

"Tomorrow will be better," Stephen said when I collapsed into bed.

"I know. I want to see rainbows!" I enthused, envisaging the spray-filled gorge lit up by the tropical sun. In the short walk to our room we had heard Mosi oa Tunya – *the smoke that thunders* – and I couldn't wait to revisit it in daylight.

But the next day, as I stepped around the corner of the hotel building, my time was up. A wave of heat rushed through me and my stomach heaved. I had no choice but to retreat to the sick bay and let the others view the Victoria Falls without me.

IN-LAWS ARRIVE

No sooner did our friends leave Zambia than the in-laws arrived. Some might describe it as pure foolishness, to have six weeks of uninterrupted visitors. I praised my efficiency – so efficient that they used the same plane, and I only had one early-morning trip out to the airport.

Built in the 1960s, heralding the new era of Zambia post-independence, Lusaka International Airport was a spacious building that reflected the architecture of the age. The departure hall was an expansive concourse with a fountain, a bronze statue of a lechwe and several rows of plastic chairs. The double-height ceiling kept it cool and the decor was functional. It was an inoffensive place to spend time waiting and a great place to people-watch: the stressed family, dragging luggage through the scanners; the group of backpackers, laughing and giggling with one another, all expecting to get their six-foot wooden giraffes onto the aeroplane; the people rushing in late having forgotten to pay their airport tax and, on being redirected to the payment office, tapping their feet impatiently in the queue. 'Departures' was a rolling sea of human life, with waves of conversation echoing round the vast chamber.

In contrast 'Arrivals' was small, cramped and void of anything entertaining. The grey tiled floor was like that of any school or public institution: unobtrusive, dull and resilient to wear and tear. A wall of glass opened out onto the drop-off zone and a colossal car park beyond. Most of this was never used but had been designed with the expectation of an expansion in air travel. About five metres inside the hall another wall of glass acted as a barrier to a pair of opaque doors, chained and padlocked fiercely until the flight had landed and disembarked.

I had left my friends in 'Departures', dashed up to the viewing area to see the plane landing and then joined the throng awaiting in 'Arrivals'. The space may have been empty of shops or services, adornments or posters (save for the screen displaying the arrivals and departures, which occasionally mirrored reality) but by the time the doors were unlocked the place was crammed with people. At that time BA brought the only direct flight from Europe which made its arrival quite a social event. Waiting patiently, we were confined by both space and time, united by a buzz of anticipation. Groups formed, chattering away, and traditionally dressed women clutched roses ready to give the traveller on his return.

I chose to stand in a space off to the side, away from the gaggle. I knew that meant I would be out of sight when the in-laws arrived, but didn't expect them to be first off the plane. I could edge closer as others left.

The doors were unlocked by removing the chain which made a terrifying clunk as it fell to the ground, like releasing a prisoner from a medieval dungeon. There was a collective gasp, a moment's silence and then a low murmur as all eyes turned to watch. Even I was hopeful. The uniformed pilot and crew marched through first, reflecting their status, wheeling their luggage smartly behind them. The crowd parted like the Red Sea before Moses, and, heads held imperiously high, they paraded through the mass of humanity and into a private bus taking them to their hotel. From then on it was a free-for-all to see who was next, though first class passengers must have had an advantage. I hung back, confident that wouldn't include my family.

From among the nondescript trickle of passengers, a white gentleman in his fifties or early-sixties emerged. Smartly dressed, he was immediately mobbed by a dozen locals. His trolley and luggage were taken by one smiling, deferential man, while around him a group of women reached out to hug and kiss him, handing him flowers. It took a while for the exhausted-looking man to make his way through the throng, shuffling forwards and greeting all the welcomers with a smile. Outside, loosening the bottleneck, the women formed a semi-circle around him. Only then did I register two things: they were all wearing the same chitenge that brightly declared their church mission, and the man was wearing a dog-collar. Then the women started singing: perfect harmony, joyful vocals praising God for the return of their pastor. They swung from side to side and danced, clapping their hands and yodelling their rhythm. The arrivals lounge vicariously shared their joy, mesmerised by the jubilation outside.

While I was staring at the pastor and his choir, my three in-laws (father-, mother- and sister-in-law) surprised me by arriving. They were much more adept at getting through passport control than we ever were.

"Welcome to Zambia!" I waved my arm to encompass the impromptu concert. "See what a show I put on for you!" I teased, taking the trolley of suitcases from Grampa and shooing away an over-eager porter. The singing followed us all the way to the car.

࿏

I poured mugs of tea then collapsed on the sofa. It was only half past nine in the morning but I felt like the day was nearly through. I thought of our friends, still somewhere over northern DRC at a guess, and wondered how they were surviving the ten-hour day-flight home. With three young children, and a proportional amount of baggage, it had been a feat simply getting out of the door.

My ten seconds of peace was disrupted first by my son demanding that I separate his Lego, and then by my conscience: I really ought to have told Grannie and Grampa that their tea was ready. I was halfway to standing up when they walked through the door. *Typical!* I thought. *Just that half-step ahead of me in being perfect.* Then I reflected that maybe their offspring were the more normal human beings, as Gwyn hadn't yet appeared.

My parents-in-law were astonishing people. After seven years of marriage to their son I had grasped their daily routine. It started with a cup of tea in a china mug at 8.15 a.m., ran through a series of timed breaks for tea or coffee, and concluded with dinner at 6.32 p.m., with the washing-up done to *The Archers*. Grannie was allergic to nuts. Grampa didn't eat raspberries, because of the seeds, nor bananas, because they weren't available during the war. They were well-seasoned travellers who travelled frustratingly light and had

38

refused to bring all the chocolate I had requested. Unlike my family (grew up, went to university, got job, got married, had children) they both had exciting lives before the responsibilities of family hit. Grampa had worked for a couple of years at the British scientific research station in the Antarctic: two years of snow and ice, and two winters of no light. Having survived (for this read 'enjoyed') this he had travelled home from the southernmost tip of South America, through Central America, the United States and ended up in Vancouver. There he had met his future wife, who also had travelled the world, with her nursing friends, in previous years. Love conquered all: children had appeared and the expansive travel had stopped, in contrast to me for whom the travel had only started after the second child was born.

And now we had brought them over to Zambia, a country untouched by their previous expeditions. I was not naïve enough to think they'd come because of me, or even Stephen: no, the draw was their grandchildren and getting their daughter settled into her new home. At some point, I realised, I'd have to inform them that we were thinking of staying longer than originally planned, keeping Matthew and Eleanor away from them for a few more years.

But not now. I handed them their tea, inviting them to sit down and unwind after their overnight flight. Gwyn sauntered in and, dropping the rest of his Lego with a clatter, Matthew ran to show her his rocket.

"Ooh! Lovely, Matthew!" she exclaimed enthusiastically.

"Aunty Gin! Aunty Gin! Watch it fly! Look!"

I smiled at his inability to say the 'w' sound in her name. "Tea, Gwyn?" I offered as a distraction.

"No thanks. Is there a Coke in the fridge?"

"Of course, help yourself."

She took the cold drink from the kitchen, my son trailing after her while extolling the virtues of his newly made spacecraft.

"Your house is just perfect," Grannie said, sipping her drink.

"Really?" I said without thinking. I knew it wasn't. I still found it gloomy and the dark brown concrete floor in every room made me miserable. The shade from the trees outside prevented any bright sunlight lightening the mood.

"The garden's perfect for Matthew and Eleanor. I bet they love running around outside."

"Yes," I laughed, "and they have the mulberry-stained clothes to prove it!"

"It is a glorious tree," Grampa said, scrutinising its thick trunk. "Do you make jam?"

I heard Gwyn snort, then hide her amusement with a cough. Sometimes I didn't think my parents-in-law knew me at all. *Do I make jam?*

"I probably ought to," I said, and changed the subject. "So, what are the plans? What do you want to do with your three weeks?"

"Well," said Grampa, "we'd thought about going to Livingstone, to the Victoria Falls, but I gather you've arranged a trip somewhere else?" He left the words hanging.

"We've booked into a lodge at South Luangwa National Park, to go on safari. It is supposed to be one of the best places in the world to see animals. But that isn't for a couple of weeks, so there's plenty of time for a trip to Livingstone."

"Other than the Falls there isn't much to do," said Gwyn. She had visited when she came for her job interviews at Easter. Her first view of the Victoria Falls was from the air: the most spectacular approach possible on a microlight. With the river in full flood it had been an awesome experience that she had, excitedly and repeatedly, told us about. Everything else on her trip had faded into insignificance.

Despondent, Grampa looked down at the table. "Perhaps we shouldn't go there then–" but Gwyn interrupted.

"No – of course you should. I just meant that you don't need to spend a long time in Livingstone. You can stay at Fawlty Towers."

I tried to hide my envy. I'd wanted to try the magnificently named Fawlty Towers but they didn't welcome children. But nothing stopped my parents-in-law. They discussed transport with Gwyn and, before I knew it, they were set on catching the bus down to Livingstone to stay in the backpackers lodge. I'd now been to Livingstone twice, driving each time (the latest trip involving all those vomit stops), and the prospect of eight hours sardined in with the locals on a smelly, dangerous bus filled me with dread. I'd overtaken so many broken-down buses, usually at dangerous corners of blind summits, that I couldn't help but expect a disaster. And then to stay in the budget décor of Fawlty Towers – could that possibly be suitable for my parents-in-law?

I watched the three of them. All exhaustion from the overnight flight had vanished as they were animated by their plans. Here I saw the difference between my husband's family and my own: mine would have been wary and cautious, whereas they were lit up by the prospect of adventure.

As was Matthew, now planning an excursion to the moon.

෨

The first week was used not only to plan the

Livingstone trip, but also to help settle Gwyn into her new job, house and country: another Withenay crossing continents and making a fresh start. It was on Gwyn's previous visit that she had secured a job teaching at the international school. I felt responsible for this, given I had seen the advert in Matthew's pre-school letter and had emailed Gwyn tongue-in-cheek that she might like to consider it. She did. She came, was interviewed and then offered a position.

Stephen had organised accommodation for her in one of the flats in our complex. She was staying with us until it was properly settled, although the first three weeks were going to be cramped. We had one spare room and double bed, which Grannie and Grampa were using. The only option for Gwyn was the lower bunk bed underneath Matthew, while Eleanor remained in her cot. I had apologised to her in case she was disturbed by them, particularly in the morning.

"I'll be fine," she had said breezily. "I sleep through most things."

Just like her elder brother, I'd thought, noting another strength in his family gene pool.

That afternoon we took a look around Gwyn's new home. I was amused watching Grampa as he toured the two-bedroomed flat. Tension mounted with each room we entered. The living room light hung with some bare wires visible near the ceiling: that would have to be dealt with. There were rips in the mosquito netting at the windows: that would have to be fixed. The bathroom tap was stiff: that would have to be loosened. Add to that the dust and grime, the ants in the kitchen, and the lime-scale coating the sinks and bath: it was a miracle he could bear the place at all.

The next morning I sent Precious over to clean, while Grampa created a checklist of corrections necessary to protect his daughter.

⮿

Watching Gwyn move house and country gave me a great sensation of déjà vu, as I recalled our first days and weeks in Zambia. It was a lot more pleasurable helping her than doing it myself. I secretly hoped that I'd never, ever be doing it again, although nothing was certain. According to the current timetable we were still due to leave within twelve months, but Stephen and I had talked. He was hopeful for a six-month extension to his research project here in Lusaka. Then the plan was for him to return to the UK to complete his qualifications and apply for a further research grant, while I would stay and wait. If all went according to plan, Stephen would be back within a year. In the interim, our stay would neatly coincide with Gwyn's two-year contract and the completion of Margriet's time in Zambia.

Meanwhile, when I wasn't at work, my week was spent running around town finding the bits to fix Gwyn's accommodation to her father's satisfaction.

"I think your dad's happy with the electrics now," I said to Stephen as we went to bed one evening. "I'm not sure what more he can do to make it safe. Anyway, they're off to Livingstone tomorrow and I'm left with a shopping list for the plumbing."

"Sorry," he mumbled. "It's Gwyn, you see."

I smiled. "I know. Daddy's girl. Got to protect her. He'd never do the same for you, eh?"

"Nope!"

I snuggled down under the duvet. No, Gwyn was the baby of the family and a girl. She'd been driven to and from university, unlike her brothers, and now she had the tender care to get her house perfect before she moved in.

"Don't forget to ask the garden boy about the netting," Stephen said as he switched off the light.

In the dark he couldn't see my smirk. "I won't," I replied. Gwyn's elder brother was every bit as protective of her as her father.

❧

Gwyn's arrival in Zambia threw in one further conundrum: how to get to and from the school. She didn't have enough money to go out and buy a car (at least not a car that her brother was prepared to let her purchase) but the commute would be a nightmare if reliant on minibuses. Like in most major cities, virtually no-one took circular routes around the city; the majority took the arterial routes into a central bus station. Gwyn would therefore have to take two buses each way, adding time even more than cost. Given Matthew went to the school every day (and it wouldn't be long before Eleanor joined him) one trip was sorted, but her working day was longer than his.

For her first week Stephen and I juggled being a taxi service, but this was not a practical long-term option. She could have The Professor to herself when we travelled to South Luangwa, but week in, week out she would need some independence. It was on thinking this through that we hit upon the idea of having a driver.

Many people and companies in Zambia employed drivers. For the company executives, this was a perk of the job, a show of status. In smaller companies drivers were essential to run the errands, substituting for the weaknesses of the postal system. All notes and letters were hand delivered, as it was the only way to be certain documents arrived. NGOs also employed a lot of drivers, as the long journeys around the country and into the needy rural areas were draining. These drivers were usually paid well, securing high wages to drive overseas-funded 4x4s.

Our budget was low – very low – but we'd always been keen to employ local people. As expats we lived a privileged and secluded life, sheltered from the worst of the local living standards. Employing people was our way of supporting the country.

Finding a driver was not straightforward. I decided it was best to go by word of mouth and so started by asking a friend how her husband found his driver. "He came with the car and the job," she replied. Embassy work had its benefits. "But he has a brother," she added.

Godfrey arrived early one morning for his interview. Stephen and I had planned a list of questions, but it was hardly a grilling.

"How old are you?"

"What grade did you reach at school?"

"Where do you live?"

"How long have you had your driving licence?"

"Do you have it with you?"

The real test was to drive the car. We had decided to let him drive Stephen to work, with me in the back as a passenger, then give him his bus fare home.

Godfrey got into the driving seat. Within a minute he had worked out which hole to put the key into. A couple of minutes later he started the engine and eventually managed to find reverse gear. Stephen helped him, by indicating we weren't going to move without the handbrake being released.

At last we were off: into the hedge. The scrape with greenery (and a rather close shave with the ditch on the other side) did not seem to deter him at all. First gear was engaged and we were away: to the gate, then onto the road. By the time we'd reached the hospital he had been bold enough to venture into third gear, but over five kilometres of untaxing roads this was exhausting. He was given his bus fare, before Stephen and I turned to look at each other.

"No," we said in unison.

The second applicant was younger, more educated and, after the interview, seemed an excellent candidate. He managed to get into reverse and out of the driveway in a timely and, more importantly, safe and confident fashion. The road was clear and the lights ahead were green, but turned to red. This didn't seem to phase him: he carried straight on, across the junction, as cars were coming from the sides. Stephen and I were terrified: that particular crossing was always a little precarious and we were usually hyper-cautious.

Not wishing to think ill of our young candidate, Stephen told him gently that he must stop at 'stop' signs and red lights. "Yes sir," he responded, and went straight across another junction with a 'stop' sign. Another candidate failing our test.

As with many Zambian structures, it appeared that the way to pass the driving test was not through a display of rigorously tested skill. Knowing the right person, or a generous donation to someone's pocket, went a long way. Both drivers so far had valid licences but would have barely left the examination centre in the UK. I worried whether we would ever find someone who could actually drive.

Before resorting to an advert in the local magazine I asked at work, with little expectation of anything better than we'd experienced, but a fellow church member was suggested. Mature, sensible and well presented, Justin drove us safely across town, with no bumps, scrapes or breaking of the law. He got the job on the spot.

Meanwhile, we had an adventure to go on. Gwyn had sole use of The Professor for a week: The Bishop, laden to the gunnels, was taking the rest of us to

Mfuwe and the South Luangwa National Park, reputedly one of the best game parks in the world. It promised to be the most amazing experience.

"IT'S A LITTLE ROUGH"

The Bishop bumped along the track out of Petauke. It was a poor excuse for a road, but over the previous year we had come to expect roads to shake us up. Perhaps Stephen was being considerate to his parents but we were going at no great speed. Five hours, the manager at our overnight lodge had said, so we had set off confidently. Even with a variety of toilet stops and food breaks that was ample time to reach our destination before nightfall and I was determined to achieve this aim on at least one long, cross-Zambia journey.

We'd chosen the short route to Mfuwe for our week of safari. Normal people took the main road to Chipata, then headed north: two sides of a triangle, if you like. Our route went via Petauke, cross-country, then followed the Luangwa River. We'd asked the man at the lodge if he knew what the road was like.

"What sort of car do you have?"

"A Pajero, 4x4."

"Oh, that should be fine," he had said confidently.

Five hours? We had already travelled for two hours and it didn't feel like we'd got anywhere. Heavily laden, The Bishop shuddered with exhaustion over the dirt road. We'd crammed the four of us (children strapped onto the folding seats at the back) and my parents-in-law inside. Though some food, child-entertainment and emergency supplies were stacked between Grannie and me on the back seat, the majority of our luggage devolved to the roof rack. Strapped above us were three suitcases, as well as a spare wheel, two diesel-filled jerry cans (bright red, bought especially for the journey), a travel cot and the tarpaulin; all tightly bound to the metal frame.

"What on earth are they growing here?" I asked, as we passed a peculiar plant. It stood about waist high, with spikes jutting out of the bush and very few leaves: just a spiky black silhouette, repeated in regular rows across the fields.

"I don't know, but it's everywhere."

We were passing field after field of the unidentifiable crop.

"And what's that white stuff?"

"What white stuff?"

I wonder about my husband's observation skills sometimes. "The stuff on the roadside. Snow?"

Were all the rattles and shakes affecting my brain? Even I knew we weren't that high above sea level, and it was a little too hot.

Grampa leaned forward to get a better look at the mystery objects. "I think it's cotton," he said and gently, as realisation fell, "I guess that these fields are full of cotton plants."

Looking more closely at the crop I saw that the

prickly plant had traces of the same fluff caught up in it. I assumed that it was past harvest time, for the fields were by no means white: more a regiment of spiky, sticky bushes.

"I can see why they used slaves to pick cotton. Your hands would be torn to shreds."

All those centuries ago, all those African people traded – robbed of the dignity and respect – in order to harvest crops like this. I thought of Sherry and Precious, my maids, and of all the jobs I asked them to do. I resolved, again, to be nicer to them. Though, in fairness, nothing I asked them to do compared to the harvesting of cotton from a cotton plant. The most dangerous job they did was switching on the cooker. On reflection I wondered if that was more risky than cotton-picking, given its bare-wire electric connection to the mains.

I wondered how the Zambians who farmed these fields today were being treated. Was there any chance that they were getting a fair wage, or was it just the same as it was on those cotton plantations of the Deep South two hundred years ago? Who would be checking up on the fair wage deals in such a remote area of a remote country in Africa?

The road didn't seem to be going anywhere other than around these never-ending fields. I peered at the large-scale map from our Zambia guidebook, but it wasn't much help. Road maps of Zambia were uncommon, particularly for the more remote areas – and undoubtedly we were remote. I hadn't seen a village or settlement for ages and had begun to hope we had accidentally missed the entrance to the Game Management Area. If we were already well inside the GMA then it was probable we'd achieve my goal of reaching Mfuwe before dark.

So it was with mixed feelings that we reached

woodland, a gate and an official who signed us in.

"Is this the road to Mfuwe?"

"Yes, Bwana." He looked inside the car, counted how many of us there were and marked his clipboard. He stood back, as if confused by our presence and glanced uneasily at the road ahead. "It is a little rough," he proffered.

It didn't look that much different to the road we'd just travelled and anyway, what choice did we have? It was lunchtime, a good couple of hours since we left Petauke, and the map indicated going back would be longer than going forwards.

The guard directed us to the left hand track and we followed the dirt road. It was little different to the previous hour, though surrounded by trees rather than cotton plants. We proceeded at a reasonable pace for a few miles, before cresting a hill ready to head down through the forest.

The road instantly disappeared. In its place was a steep, rocky track. Stephen's slow speed snailed into second gear. All conversation ceased in mutual support, as if we were each in the driver's seat, each concentrating wholeheartedly on the driving. Even the children were silent. The Bishop lurched from side to side as Stephen avoided the worst of the rocks.

"What did the guard say? 'A bit rough'?"

There was a sudden jolt as a wheel hit an unexpected lump of stone.

"Careful, Stephen!" I cried out. It was less than six months since we had destroyed The Bishop's suspension on a piece of dirt road going to Kafue National Park. This was its first real test since and I had no desire to have to repair it again.

The destruction of the road was evidently the result of the rains thundering down the hillside into the basin below, seeking the quickest, easiest route. At the foot of the valley there were just rocks and a wooden bridge that we had to trust but, it being at least four months since it last rained, there was no river underneath. Tentatively we navigated the crossing, grateful for the smooth planks. The Bishop steadied herself momentarily, before she was thrust into the steep incline on the other side of the valley over similar, water-ruined roads.

The journey seemed to go on forever, wiggling through trees and the miombo woodland. When we reached a more recently graded piece of road, we accelerated to maybe thirty kilometres per hour.

"It feels like we're flying," I said, as we raced along. Then I voiced my main concern. The steep valley passage had slowed us down considerably. "Do you think we'll get there before dark?"

"I'm sure," said Stephen, before adding more cautiously, "if it stays like this…"

"Do you ever arrive anywhere before nightfall?" Grampa asked.

I considered whether to lie. "No," I admitted reluctantly. "Still, we can't be far off now. We're looking out for a road coming in from the left, and then for the Luangwa River, which we'll follow all the way up to the lodge."

A little further on I wondered if I was hallucinating, having been cooped up in a vehicle for hours. I was sure I could smell diesel, and feared that the engine had broken in some way, allowing the fumes to permeate the inside of The Bishop. I sniffed (subtly, so as not to offend my mother-in-law next to me) which just confirmed the smell. Turning to look out of the window I discovered the reason. A light brown smear covered the glass.

"Oh heck! Stephen!"

"Yes?"

"We have a problem."

"In what way?"

"Well, I think there's diesel leaking down over my door."

Grannie looked across. "So there is," she said incredulously.

Stephen stopped the car and walked round to my side to inspect. "Oh," he said, looking at the window then lifting his eyes to the roof. "Oh," he said again.

Grampa joined him and together they assessed the situation. Frustratingly, I couldn't hear what was said. They had stepped away from the vehicle and I didn't dare open the window for fear of being dripped on.

"Are we there, Mummy?" asked Matthew.

I turned to speak to him. "No, we've just got a problem with one of the diesel cans on the roof. It'll be all that bumping around we've been doing."

"Bump! Bump!" Eleanor demonstrated, with a giggle.

Stephen stuck his head into the car to ask for a water bottle, confirming at the same time that the brown drips all emanated from one of my nice, new, red plastic fuel cans. The plan was to take all the luggage off the roof rack to see what damage we'd incurred and (most importantly) to remove the fuel can.

Unbeknown to me, we had stopped not only in the middle of a road in the middle of a forest in the middle of nowhere, but next to a group of traditional huts arced around a community shelter. We had drawn the attention of the local villagers and a group of men came to lend us a hand.

Stephen took the offending plastic container (it was cursed repeatedly, "Cheap import", "Waste of money", "Should've known better") down from the luggage rack and the nifty pouring device that had persuaded me to buy it (more curses) was used to empty the leftover diesel into our half-empty fuel tank. One man from the village crawled around underneath with a bowl to catch the extra drips. More time was consumed as the luggage was re-jigged and re-roped onto the roof rack.

Grannie and I rummaged around in the remains of our picnic and pulled out some oranges as a thank you to the villagers. They were most grateful: uncomfortably so, given it was the excess from our ample lunch. Stephen offered them the empty red fuel can – now useless and of no value to us – and they also saved a bowlful of fuel from the drips as it was emptied into the tank. Quite possibly that was the most valuable gift they received.

Still, although time had been lost in our race to reach Mfuwe before nightfall, no great damage had been done. We had lost a fuel can, but saved the majority of the fuel. Thankfully, the road was less challenging than before and we maintained a good speed over the sandy track.

The lengthening journey had resulted in yet another round of the tape singing, "The wheels on the bus go round and round." I knew these songs back-to-front and inside-out, as Matthew insisted on listening to them every time he got into the car. Just as I was about to throw a tantrum myself about the repetitive music Grannie (the world's most amazing carer of under-fives) stepped in with some extra verse suggestions.

"How about some animals, for a change? What animals could we have on the bus?"

I imagine she was expecting to hear cow ("goes moo, moo, moo!"), sheep ("baaa!"), dog, horse, hen or even a cockerel ("cockadoodle doo!"), and had to admire her for being unfazed by Matthew's response.

"A crocodile!"

We all sang lustily. "The crocodile on the bus goes snap, snap, snap!" with accompanying actions and many giggles. A proliferation of jungle animals then followed, emphasising to Grannie that her grandchildren were not being brought up in the English countryside.

At long last the tape was switched off and (despite the singing) a more peaceful atmosphere filled the car.

"Stephen..."

"Yes," he replied warily.

"I keep hearing this rattling noise from overhead. Is the roof rack OK?"

"We tied everything up securely. I can't believe anything could be moving," he said.

"OK." I was assuaged briefly, but the rattle persisted. Now the rest of the family commented too, so Stephen pulled over once more to take a look.

"The bolts have worn a little loose," he said, reaching into the car for the toolkit. Together with his father they tightened the bolts that held the rack to the frame on the car. Thus secured, Stephen started up once more.

We had no idea where we were. The milometer gave an indication of how far we'd come, but the distance to Mfuwe was interpolation and guesswork. The children were more and more fidgety and being pacified with titbits of food. Grannie did a marvellous job reading stories to keep them occupied, or playing simple observation games. 'I-spy' in the Zambian bush was quite limited though. (Tree. Bush. Grass. Sky. Sun.) Allegedly, our road had followed the line of the Lusangazi River, a tributary of the Luangwa River, but I had seen no evidence of running water.

At the sight of a group of huts I was delighted. We were approaching the lodges that line the Luangwa valley and thus the beginning of civilisation. I had been clinging to the hope of seeing Chichele Lodge which, though not our destination, was the first in a long string of lodges along the river bank (according to the map).

In my experience lodges were better signposted than anything else and if we could reach just one I would feel safe.

The local children were running around, waving at us. We slowed down, stopping beside a couple of elderly gentlemen. As if from nowhere the children were at the window, begging for sweets. Grannie and I hunted for something to give them, but we had consumed most of our nibbles as the day had progressed. So much for the five-hour estimate: we had been on the road for over seven already.

Stephen spoke to the gentlemen.

"How far is it to Mfuwe?"

One of them smiled a toothless grin and nodded, as if he understood everything, but then made it clear that he understood nothing. His compatriot had a little English.

"Four kilometre," he stumbled out, heavily accented.

"Thank you," Stephen replied. "Thank you. Have a good day." With a cheery wave we left their village. *Four kilometres! Not far to go now!*

Six kilometres on there was no indication we were any closer to Mfuwe. The road looked the same. The countryside looked the same. Our newfound confidence had vanished.

We looked for signs of life, like fresh green leaves on trees that might indicate we were approaching the Luangwa River. There was hope, as we headed straight towards a coppice, then the road suddenly dropped down a short incline. Ahead of us was the 'river' for certain: a wide valley where water should flow, and no doubt did at other times of the year. We were faced with large white boulders, one car width only, stretching over to the other side.

This was not a road: this was an assault course.

Cautiously Stephen drove The Bishop across the

rocky embankment. Despite the odd uncomfortable scraping noise, we reached the other side. Our hopes that we were close to our destination were dashed yet again when we reached another riverbed crossing, identical to the first. I wondered whether we were just going round in circles.

At the next village we asked again how far it was to Mfuwe.

"Eighty kilometres," the man said.

Eighty? This did nothing to improve our morale.

Once again we started the car and moved on, following the interminable road.

All of a sudden we came to the Lusangazi Gate, one of the two entrances to South Luangwa National Park. It was a great relief, for finally we knew we were on the map: not yet at the lodges, but hopeful we would reach someone who could rescue us with food and drink and the promise of a bed for the night.

Our journey now took on a much more positive vibe, as we could excite the children (and ourselves) by looking out for animals. We were driving parallel to the river and, though not in the park itself, we were in a GMA where the animals were protected by consent, if not by law. The animals, of course, had no clue about the placement of our human boundaries. It was known that the elephants liked to leave the park and cross the river at night so they could raid the locals' fields for food. Clearly an entire nine thousand square kilometres of wilderness and protection was not enough for them.

"Who can be first to spot a lion?" Stephen called from the front of the car.

"Or a tiger!" suggested Grampa.

"Or a penguin!" said Matthew.

I didn't hold out much hope for my family.

As we crept onwards to Mfuwe I saw the sign for Chichele Lodge and my heart soared with delight.

Finally I felt able to relax. There were copious rattles and bumps from The Bishop, but now I accepted them as normal. She (my Bishop was definitely female) had had a strenuous day. The end was in sight. Behind us was the setting sun, turning the sky a glorious shade of orange and coating the landscape with its golden glow. Somewhere out there were lions and leopards, impala and puku, giraffe and zebra, all waiting to be found. I shut my eyes and dreamt of my imminent gin and tonic.

There was a whooshing noise. Stephen exclaimed, "Oh no!" and drew to a suspiciously quiet stop. In unison, we slowly turned round and looked out of the back window.

There, lying in the middle of the road, was our roof rack.

MFUWE MAGIC

Stephen reversed The Bishop while we all stared out of the rear window at the neat package.

"It looked like a flying carpet," he said. "I could see it in the wing mirror – floating off on a current, landing on the ground."

We continued to stare, imagining the delicacy of its descent.

"On the positive side," Grampa observed, "all the luggage is still attached."

There was a further moment of reverent silence before Stephen said, "Right! Better go see what we can do!"

While Stephen and his father went to examine the roof rack, I climbed out to stretch my legs. A movement in the undergrowth reminded me of where we were. *Lions*, I thought. I scanned the brown grasses for any sign of animals and double-checked that the boulders in the distance weren't really elephants. Then I told the children, very firmly, that they were to stay in the car and under no circumstances whatsoever were they to move.

The men's inspection of rack and Bishop revealed that the metal was shorn right through and there was no way we could reattach the rack to the bars on the car. We had no choice but to unpack the rack (again), cram our belongings into the car and return for the metal rack in the morning.

"Right kids!" I said cheerily to them. "It's going to be a bit of a squeeze. Can we put all your bits and pieces back in your bags first."

Matthew dutifully passed me some books and toy cars, but clung steadfastly to Teddy. Eleanor, of course, didn't understand what I was asking but nevertheless passed me her doll. In a flash of parental responsibility, brought on by the worry that I couldn't remember the last time I'd done it, I also seized the opportunity for a quick nappy-change.

Somehow we forced the two huge suitcases into the boot of the car, though Matthew and Eleanor were barely visible anymore. Grannie and I sat in the back, cuddling rucksacks and divided by a wall of bags.

Stephen and Grampa dragged the empty rack, together with the spare wheel and the second, empty diesel can, to a distinctive baobab tree by the side of the road and, once we had wedged David into the front seat with our remaining belongings, we got on our way. Meanwhile, my dream of arriving at our lodge before sunset sank behind the skyline.

❧

A dozen large tables filled the wide terrace, laid as if for a wedding banquet: starched serviettes and sizeable dinner plates, sparkling wine glasses of various sizes. Above, the sky was ink-black, studded with diamond stars. The air was heavy yet fresh, as the dust of the day settled into the balm of the night. A log fire crackled and spat in one corner, opposite a swimming pool that edged the vertical drop to the river valley below. Behind and to the right was a buffet table laden with salads; to the left, desserts. There was a pleasant hum of conversation as guests, dressed for dinner, were guided by waiters to their table.

Into this tranquil scene dropped our frazzled family of six in day-long crumpled clothing and carrying the faint aroma of diesel. I was seated next to an impeccably presented lady who had no doubt spent a king's ransom on her dream safari holiday and didn't expect such riffraff in a place like this.

"Hello," she said. "How are you?"

She did well not to wrinkle her nose.

"Fine." My befuddled brain had reached capacity and I was struggling to find the right words to respond. A polite, "And you?" would have sufficed but most of my effort was concentrated on sitting upright and smiling.

"Have you travelled far?" she asked.

"From Lusaka." I'd picked up on her American tones and had the presence of mind to wonder if she knew where that was. "I assume by your accent you've come from the States. Whereabouts?"

"New York."

"Lucky you! What do you do there?"

She took a forkful of salad. "I read the news on TV."

I'm not sure if there was any other response she could have made that would have floored me so completely. I had to give her a good look to see if I recognised her. I didn't, but then my repertoire of American newsreaders was small. She was certainly beautiful, slim in safari khaki with long blonde hair tied back in a ponytail. I was jerked back to reality when I realised I hadn't heard her next question. She repeated it patiently.

"What have you seen today?"

What had I seen today? Trees? Road?

Then the fog lifted. She meant what *animals* had I seen. Presumably she had just returned from an evening safari viewing the wildlife: the antelope, zebra and warthog, the giraffe and hippos. She probably would have had a sundowner that involved gin and tonic, not rescuing flying roof racks.

I hadn't seen any animals. Thank goodness.

"We've only just arrived," I told her. "It was quite a journey."

࿔

I spent the next morning sorting through our belongings. One of our suitcases had been badly soaked with diesel and had an unpleasant stain across one corner. The contents hadn't fared much better. I put all the diesel-stained clothes into a wicker basket to be collected and washed by the lodge staff, then tried to give the case a good scrub. A paperback had to be abandoned completely, another was having a stay of execution and I was grateful that the waterproof lining on my wash bag had saved my toothbrush.

While I undertook this unsavoury task, Grannie took Matthew and Eleanor to explore the lodge's facilities. Stephen and Grampa ventured out again in The Bishop, returning to the baobab tree to retrieve our broken roof rack.

Baobabs, renowned for their distinctive shape, are

spread across Africa. The *Adansonia* (to give it its scientific name) is named after the French botanist Michel Adanson who gave the name baobab to the fruit, and then the tree. The stout trunk, a smooth purplish-grey, can be up to ten metres in diameter and from the top sprout branches like roots, hence it is often described as the 'upside down tree'. The tale is told that the baobab was first planted in the Congo basin, where it complained of excessive dampness. God was so angered by its constant wailing that he plucked it up and threw it into a dry area, where it landed upside down.

According to Zambian folklore the baobab started out as a creeper that coiled itself around a tree, engulfed it and turned it into a baobab. Local custom also thought that sucking or eating the seeds was not a good idea, as it attracted crocodiles. We decided not to test that theory out.

Due to their enormous girth it is thought that baobabs live to a great age. The Shiramba tree in Mozambique is thought to be over 2000 years old. It was formerly known as the Livingstone Tree and his initials were found carved inside the trunk, though there is an irony to this. David Livingstone, the great explorer, had been furious with Adanson after he'd suggested that there were baobab trees over 5150 years old. Livingstone was of the religious opinion that the world was created by God in 4004 BC, so such an age of tree placed it as growing before Noah, thus questioning the Flood and biblical truth.

Despite all this furore, the trees are difficult to age as the trunk is largely hollow and fibrous, thus absorbing water and expanding during rains, but also shrinking during periods of drought. The hollowing of trunks has been used for a wide variety of ingenious purposes, though. They are a natural way to store water and useful in drought-stricken areas since a medium sized tree could hold as much as four hundred gallons. Trunks have also been used as tombs, particularly for those denied burial and who are 'caught between the earth and the sky'. They have variously been used as meeting places, a prison, stables, to house a weaver's loom, a bus shelter, a watchtower, a shed for storing garden implements and as a cool room for a bar. Most unique is the baobab at Katimo Mulilo, far to the west of Zambia, which was fitted out by a Major Trollip. Reputedly he was so bored at his outpost with nothing to do that he instructed his staff to install a flush toilet.

I had nearly completed sifting out and cleaning our diesel-stained belongings when Stephen came back from the baobab. He'd left The Bishop and the roof rack with the lodge mechanics.

"What did they say?" I asked.

"Well, they asked what had happened, and I explained about the rattling, the flying and then leaving the rack by the baobab overnight.

"'On the road west?' they asked.

"'Yes,' I replied, and they frowned and tutted.

"'That is a bad tree,' they said. 'Bees.'"

Stephen drew breath.

"Bees?" I queried.

"Apparently the tree is dangerously full of them. That, and snakes," Stephen replied. "Still, they said they would do what they could to repair The Bishop and will let us know."

I shook my head. "How did we survive that journey?" I asked, without expecting a reply. All I could do was hope that the mechanics would fix our roof rack, because I wasn't at all sure how we'd manage the long journey home without it.

Meanwhile, we had a holiday to enjoy. Time to put the flying roof rack to the back of our minds.

છે

We had five days at the lodge, filled with early morning game drives (leaving shortly after 6 a.m.) and late evening meals. Most guests just passed through for a couple of nights, some going further into the park to stay at bush camps. I didn't see my American newsreader friend again. As a family we alternated the evening game drives with my parents-in-law: if remaining in camp, the job was to feed the children and put them to bed; if out in the bush, the aim was to see a leopard.

Stephen and I had many objectives before we left Zambia, but our main non-work-related priority was to see the 'Big Five' – elephant, rhino, buffalo, lion and leopard. The 'Big Five' sobriquet arose not because of their physical size but because they are reputed to be the five most difficult animals to hunt on foot – difficult because of their risk to human life. Our shots were just with a camera and (ideally) from the back of a Landcruiser, rather than marching through the savanna grasslands.

My favourite, the elephant, although instantly recognisable is surprisingly easy to hide in grassland or bushy area. Prone to charging when upset or angered, the sharp tusks would cause more than enough damage. If they didn't, its stomping feet and enormous weight would finish the deed. I delighted in seeing family herds crossing the Luangwa River, climbing down the sandy embankments with remarkable grace.

The rhinoceros is similarly troublesome and temperamental, though there were none in South Luangwa National Park. To truly hunt "The Big Five" one would chase down the black rhinoceros, but they are frighteningly close to extinction throughout Africa, with only a few hundred remaining at time of writing. We had been fortunate to see a white rhinoceros when travelling with our friends in Livingstone, guided there by its twenty-four-hour guard. He had been keen for us to edge closer and closer, so we could take a really good photo. With five children under the age of five between us we had been terrified. Still, rhino had been ticked off our list.

South Luangwa is, however, littered with Cape buffalo. These peculiar-looking creatures live in vast herds. A toss and a flick from their short, spiked horns is enough to kill anyone. Reputedly they kill more humans than any other animal (apart from humans themselves), though I have heard the same said about hippos and the biggest man-killer (if you count them as animals) is undoubtedly the mosquito. Despite a similar appearance, Cape buffalo should not be confused with buffalo that provide milk for our consumption: they would not appreciate your intimacy with them, and you would not appreciate their response.

It only took one game drive to spot the elephant and buffalo, but the two big cats were more of a challenge. The lion is well known and comparatively easy to track down, particularly as they live socially in prides. Unlike many animals they will attack even if unprovoked, thereby making it the most fearsome to meet on foot.

Knowing we were searching for lions, our guide got a tip-off from one of the other drivers. We raced across the park to see two lionesses. They were a sorry sight.

"They were not good hunters," our guide informed us. "They had not eaten for a long time. They were hungry."

So hungry that they'd resorted to catching a porcupine. Their mouths were pierced by its needles and the lionesses were waiting to die.

Being a stereotypical tourist, and worried that I

might never see another lion, I snapped away with the camera. A lost moment of concentration, though, led to Eleanor dropping her juice cup on the ground beside the Landcruiser. I was instantly in a quandary. It was the only one I had left that didn't leak all over the place, and she refused to drink out of a standard glass. I made to jump down to pick it up, but the guide shouted, "No!" and started the engine.

Gingerly, he steered the vehicle around and crept down to retrieve the bottle, out of sight of the poorly cats. I didn't think they had the energy left to pounce, but the guide wasn't taking the chance. You do not make large movements when in the presence of lions, even if they're dying.

The most elusive of the 'Big Five' but, for us, the icing on the cake was the leopard. It is a surprisingly small creature (about knee high to a man), largely nocturnal and solitary, except when mating or raising a cub. Its usual fare is antelope, which it then drags up into a tree to prevent other carnivores from stealing its catch. Their rosette skin pattern camouflages them perfectly in trees, where they usually lie on the branches during the day. At night they stalk the savanna.

Matthew's excitement grew with each drive we took, taking on a personal quest to find a leopard despite the improbability of seeing one in daylight hours. The chances were slim in the evening when they were active, but negligible during the day. On the evening game drives Stephen and I travelled in anticipation. Every time we returned disappointed.

Nevertheless, our morning and evening rides opened our eyes to a plethora of wildlife and its habitat. If I hadn't been smitten already, this was the break that cemented my love of Zambia. There was nothing quite like being in the bush. It was nature at its rawest, a place where you could almost touch the past, the way the world was created. Just the sight of trees rubbed to a shine by warthog or scratched by monkeys was exciting. A waterhole was a mecca for animals, drawn to the life-giving water, yet could also be their doom, as giraffes were snapped by crocodiles. In the bush humans were not in complete control: every trip was a risk, as we could not predict what animal we would find around the corner.

The most amazing part was how invisible the animals were. Take zebra, for example, with their distinctive black and white stripes. Nearing the end of the dry season the tree trunks were brown, the dust was reddish-brown, even the leaves were barely hinting at green. And yet zebra were so difficult to spot. If large animals could be camouflaged so well, how much more so for smaller ones, such as bush babies, voles or shrews, yet our guides were skilled at pointing out all varieties of animal life.

The countryside was a mix of wooded areas and open savanna. The low brown grass and bushy trees could easily hide a pride of lions. Puku and impala with their stripy bottoms wandered between the bushes and grasses, horns poking up to identify them from their surrounds. Our guides were experts. A combination of having been raised in the valley, where they needed to know about the habits of animals in order to survive, and passing strict exams to qualify for the job meant their knowledge of wildlife was second to none. They could follow the tracks of a leopard across many square kilometres of parkland and see the smallest, brownest of birds in the most deeply wooded areas.

The birds were another eye-opener for me. My favourites for their colour and vibrancy were the lilac-breasted roller bird and the bee-eaters. The bee-eaters were sociable, darting in and out of their sandy riverbank nests, perching on the neighbouring trees and bushes, then flocking back. Their bright colours brought a smile to everyone's face and sent the cameras clicking into overtime. In contrast the lilac-breasted roller bird was a lonesome creature, perched high on a tree. Its wings were luminescent, catching the sunlight way up high, like a piece of bright silk floating on the wind.

I loved these birds for their colour, but for sheer majestic power and beauty the winner had to be the fish eagle. It was Zambia's national bird, as seen on the flag, and a distinctive sight by the river. Black and white, it rested on a branch at the top of a tree, silhouetted against the sky, which made it easy to spot from a distance as we were driving around. It watched the river, looking for its lunch, then – on some movement that was impossible to discern with our eyes – it swooped down, touched the water with its claws and rose high into the air again, fish held tightly in its talons.

Seeing this, the way nature worked so naturally and beautifully, made me aware of how sanitised humans in developed nations had become. We did the same every day – work, in order to eat, in order to survive. Somehow our predilection for battery farming or a factory line of animals for the slaughter doesn't have the same beauty or gravitas. Perhaps I am too romantic, but the natural hunt of prey was spellbinding.

≈

Stephen and I spent the last evening packing while our children slept. We'd done the equivalent of tossing a coin for who would get the final night drive. As our guests, Grannie and Grampa won. They were willing to stay and look after the children, but we insisted they took the opportunity while they could. We lived in Zambia so no doubt there would be other occasions for us to go on safari drives. Besides, we could enjoy a relatively quiet evening before the long journey home. The lodge mechanics informed us midweek that they'd fixed The Bishop, in that the roof rack had been welded back onto the brackets. Nevertheless, I was concerned about the drive home. Would the rack hold over the bumps and twists of the six hundred kilometre journey?

A lodge employee came to babysit outside our chalet while we went for our final meal on the terrace. It remained like a Hollywood film set, but at long last we had managed to unwind and appreciate the beauty of our surrounds. We met Grannie and Grampa there, refreshed after their night drive. I was quite disappointed this would be our last restaurant meal for some time.

"Was it a good drive?" I asked, tucking into the fresh salad.

"Oh yes," Grannie said, with a twinkle in her eye. She looked radiant, as if she'd had a thoroughly wonderful time. "Yes, it was lovely."

Grampa chipped in. "We saw lots of animals – you know, the usual: buffalo, warthog, giraffe, zebra, the hippos…"

Then the reason for Grannie's delight became clear.

"And a leopard," she said.

HOMEWARD BOUND

I'd worried about our return journey but sensibly we (like the Wise Men) returned by a different route – the route we should have taken in the first place. Within yards of leaving Mfuwe village the smooth tarmac that had been laid for the tourists disappeared and once again we were on a dirt road. I held my breath, praying that the roof rack would hold, but this was not like the road in from Petauke. It had been graded recently and was comfortably wide enough for cars and lorries to pass. A few stretches were washerboard in style – a raft of ridges that shook us up – but the majority were well levelled. And the roof rack held firm.

It was a wonderful opportunity to see the wide-ranging beauty of life in Zambia. We had been spoilt by the riches of the wildlife in South Luangwa National Park, but from the car we caught glimpses of real, rural life.

We slowed down to drive through a village, clearly a sizeable point en route to Chipata. There was nothing so grand as a petrol station but there were a few shops on the roadside and some market stalls selling vegetables. Ladies sat behind their stalls: planks of wood resting on stones. Tomatoes were stacked perfectly: enticing red balls balanced in pyramids. People milled about, watching the vehicles passing. Children were kicking a ball, though as we got closer we could see it was a tightly bound bundle of plastic bags. A herd of goats gave us cool stares and, on the outskirts of the settlement, we saw chickens running around between the houses, pecking at the dirt on the ground. I wondered how they survived, as there could be little in the way of nutrition in the reddish-brown dust, even for a chicken.

We overtook a small, turquoise van driven by an old gentleman trundling along at little over fifteen kilometres per hour. He smiled and greeted us with a wave as we sped past. The old man's wrinkled face was so content and happy, and his generous, heartfelt gesture put a big grin on my face. We waved back cheerily and soon accelerated out of the village. The landscape returned to miombo woodland: low brush and scrubland spreading out over the hills.

"Uh-oh," I said.

"What?" Stephen asked from the passenger seat.

"I don't want to worry you…" Stephen now looked petrified "… but we don't appear to have any fuel."

Stephen's eyebrows nearly hit the roof. "What?"

It was a little incongruous, given we were happily speeding along at about a hundred kilometres per hour, and I knew we'd filled up before leaving Mfuwe, but the gauge was on "E": well and truly empty.

Stephen leant over to look. "So it is," he said, as if I

would lie about it.

I tapped the dashboard, hoping that the dial had got stuck or something, but it made no difference. I glanced at Stephen and took a big deep breath. "I'll find somewhere to stop so we can have a look."

We pulled over under the first tree I could find. We were on the wrong side of the road for it to cast much morning shade but the leafy branches provided a little respite from the sun while the men, once more, got out to look at the damage to The Bishop.

There was no evidence of a leak, no trails of fuel on the road behind The Bishop. Stephen unscrewed the fuel cap and peered into the tank. "I can't see anything," he said, before acknowledging that this proved nothing, as even when full it was rare to see any fuel at the lip of the tank. "I wonder if we can hear anything?"

He and Grampa shook the car at the back, testing its suspension once more.

"Whoa! Careful!" I called. "There's a fully laden roof rack, you know!"

I got a look from my husband. "It's been through worse on the drive to get here," he reminded me. "Anyway, we could hear fuel. There's definitely something in there sloshing about."

The old man in his little chugga-chugga drove past, the same big smile on his face, waving and nodding kindly at us. We waved back, though a little less cheerfully.

A spare bit of rope was found and poked into the fuel tank. It didn't take long to find liquid and when pulled out was covered in diesel. Evidently we had fuel, and probably plenty of it. Stephen screwed the cap back on.

"Start the engine again, see if that's fixed it."

The delight with old vehicles is that sometimes things just fix of their own accord, like remedying a technical problem by switching the computer off and then on again. I turned on the engine, watching the dashboard closely.

"Sorry – nothing. The gauge hasn't shifted from 'E'."

Stephen and Grampa scratched their heads, but there was little more they could do. They wiped down the piece of rope, firstly on the grass and then with tissue, before putting it in the back of the car and climbing in.

"Well," said Stephen, "there's clearly fuel there. We can't have run out – how far are we from Mfuwe?"

"Seventy, eighty kilometres?" I guessed from the milometer.

Stephen checked the map for distances and confirmed my worst fears. "About halfway." No nearer to go back than to go on. "We'll just have to head to Chipata and hope. It must be the gauge that has gone: that whatever it is inside the fuel tank and measures the quantity left has come loose and fallen off or broken going over a bump."

I must have made an audibly sharp intake of breath. "We'll be fine," he added reassuringly.

The logical part of my brain knew that they had done everything they could, but the logical part of my brain doesn't always have control over my thoughts and panicky nervous system. I stared at the fuel gauge, willing it to autocorrect, but no. We were on our way with, as far as we could tell, close to a full tank of fuel but no certainty it would stay that way. If something awful were to happen and the tank sprang a leak we would never know.

At least, not until we rolled to a stop.

The drive was now taken more gingerly. I was less confident about the bumps and twists of the road and much more keen to be economical with fuel. For a brief period we tried switching off the air-conditioning, as we knew this increased The Bishop's fuel consumption. We opened the windows, but the heat was unbearable. Right at the back of the car the children were pinned to their seats by the force of wind. They complained vociferously, and the air-conditioning was switched back on.

The journey was full of false hopes: long stretches of road... *Surely Chipata is just in front of us?*... then a bend, then more straight sections leading over undulating hills to infinity.

"Miles and miles of bloody Zambia," said my mother-in-law.

"I beg your pardon?" her son exclaimed. I'm not sure I'd ever heard her swear before.

"Miles and miles of bloody Zambia," she repeated. "It is what the guidebook said. MMBZ. I must get a photo."

"MMBZ? What – the roads just stretching on for ever?"

"Yes. Endless roads, same scenery, nothing changing. MMBZ."

I looked around. She had a point. The landscape could have been painted by Matthew: brown stripe for road, green tree blobs on either side, blue sky on top. It hadn't changed much for miles. Turning a corner onto a particularly long stretch of MMBZ, I pulled over for a photo shoot.

Grannie got out of the car and walked a few yards in front to snap away with her camera: photos of nothing but a long and dusty road, lined with miombo woodland. It was flat and monotonous, shades of dark green as the trees stretched on and on, blanketing the hillside and contrasting only with the brilliant blue sky above. It had a sense of tedium, endlessness, even perhaps hopelessness. It matched my anxiety about the journey. Lunch in Chipata, a busy town (that sold fuel), still seemed a long way away.

༚

I glanced at the clock. 16.30. Less than two hours until it would be dark and still no sign of Luangwa Bridge and our lodgings for the night. Once again, we were cutting it fine to arrive before dark. Undoubtedly the scenery was beautiful: less undulating hills, more mountainous crags; less miombo woodland, more village life or intriguing rocky outcrops. But the sun was setting and we were travelling westwards. I pulled down the visor to avoid squinting at the glare from the road.

"Everybody all right in the back there?" I called, peering in the rear-view mirror to see what the family were up to.

"Yes," they called back, in a weary tone. It had been another long day and we were all wishing for it to end.

I was still anxious about the fuel situation, despite having filled The Bishop at both Chipata and Petauke. The big "E" glared at me every time I glanced at the dashboard. There had been a brief debate about whether to stop first for lunch or to fill up the diesel. I'd been driving, so the diesel had won.

We'd had our lunch in a guesthouse a little off the main street of Chipata. The bright, clean dining area had a dozen tables covered with plastic tablecloths in floral designs, though we had been the only people there. By the entrance stood a standard plastic water container, with tap and a small bucket below, for washing our hands before eating.

The menu had been simple: rice or nshima; beef, fish or chicken relish.

"Grampa, you going to have some nshima?" I'd asked, encouraging him to try the local fare.

"No!" had come the abrupt reply. I was silenced, but Stephen laughed.

"Need to use your fingers, eh, Dad?"

"I'm having rice, with beef," he'd said pointedly, "and a fork."

I'd forgotten how Grampa couldn't abide getting his fingers sticky, and nshima was definitely a hands-on food. Of course, I couldn't let him get away so easily with this.

"Are you sure you don't want to try nshima?" I'd said. "You can't leave Africa without trying it."

"I've had it already, thank you," he'd replied, looking at me over his glasses, "and once is quite enough."

I backed off. It is best to know when you are defeated. "Fine! Rice it is."

It was fortunate that we'd shared portions as Stephen was presented with half a chicken alongside his mound of nshima. Not even the children could face the thought of ice-cream afterwards and, rather more rotund than when we arrived, we'd left Chipata with plenty of time for the rest of the journey.

Or at least, that was what I had thought. Perhaps it is just my nature to drive slowly? Since Chipata the road had been quite reasonable, with decent tarmac and only the odd stretch where I had to dance around the potholes. And yet it felt like the day was drawing to a close and we were still far from our overnight lodge. I sped up a shade, anxious to arrive before dark. We were well past Petauke and this section had held no nasty surprises on the way to Mfuwe, so I settled back confidently to enjoy the final stretch.

Out of the blue there was an explosion. The Bishop veered across the other carriageway. Terrified, I braked, stopping on the gravelly tarmac at the far side of the road.

Silence. I released the breath I didn't realise I'd been

holding.

"I think we've burst a tyre." Still clinging to the steering wheel I looked at Stephen. "Spare tyre?"

"On the roof." He smiled. "Well done on stopping."

I gave a nervous laugh. "Didn't have much choice!"

Once more Stephen and his father were out of the car and fiddling about with the luggage and the roof rack. Once more, Grannie was telling the children not to worry and finding them something to keep them occupied.

I surveyed the damage. There was a long, black line streaking across the road ending at our front wheel. The rubber had fully blown and I sighed, not sure whether I was more upset about the expense of the replacement tyre or the hassle of getting it repaired.

"Thank goodness this didn't happen on the way to Luangwa," said Stephen as he rolled the spare along.

"Thank goodness there was nothing coming the other way just now!" I exclaimed. I was still shaky, realising that we were probably only alive because the road was free of vehicles. Had another car, or worse still, a lorry, been coming the other way we might all have been written off.

Stephen opened the back doors. "Sorry kids!" he said, but they were absorbed in books. Our roadside adventures were evidently becoming mundane to them. He reached under the seat to pull out the jack and then found the toolbox wedged between Matthew and the back door. Grannie got out of the car, but the children, tightly strapped at the back of the vehicle, remained inside, which at the very least eradicated the risk of them running into the road.

Back at the wheel, we had company. There was a ridge along the edge of the road, a mound of earth that presumably was established when the highway was first cut through the hills. There had been no sign of life for miles, yet from the other side of this mound a group of local lads appeared, offering to help.

This was our third tyre blow-out since living in Zambia. The first, which happened as I was driving my father from the airport and just outside where I worked, was fixed by a driver from the office. The second was a slow deflation overnight following a particularly bumpy journey cross-country to the Kafue National Park and was fixed by mechanics at the lodge. This one, however, was ours alone to rectify.

At first Stephen and Grampa seemed keen to manage on their own, but when Stephen was under the car trying (and seemingly failing) to find where to put the jack, one of the locals stepped in to help. Shuffling under the car on his back he pointed out where it should go. From then on Gideon (as I learned he was called) proved invaluable. Having always relied on others to change the tyres it was a shock to discover just how tightly the bolts were screwed. Gideon gave added strength to the torque as the bolts were loosened and the damaged wheel removed. This man, living and working in a small rural village, had immense strength in his wiry body. There must have been nothing but muscle on him: there was certainly no fat to be seen.

But Gideon's real value, and that of his friends, came when putting on the replacement wheel. Having taken away the burst tyre, the spare wheel was rolled up, only to find there was not enough height above the ground to set it on the axle. The jack could lift The Bishop enough for a flat tyre, but a fully inflated tyre was too much. The problem was exacerbated by a slope in the road surface.

"I bought the size of jack they told me to!" I said defensively.

"Nobody's blaming you, Catharine. It's just that we have to raise the car higher." Stephen was scrambling about under the car again to check that the jack was in the right place. It was, or at least there was nowhere better.

At this point Gideon indicated that he would lift the car.

"But it's too heavy," said Stephen. "Two tonnes. Too heavy to lift."

But Gideon was insistent. "We lift!" he said, indicating his friends as well.

Reluctantly Stephen agreed, given there were now half-a-dozen young men hanging around, all nodding in support of Gideon. They stood at the front of the car while Stephen held the replacement wheel. Grampa was deputed to watch the jack, for when the car was set down again.

"OK – everyone ready?" Stephen remained anxious.

"Yes, sir!" Even in the bush there was polite deference to the white male.

"Right, after three. One. Two. Three!"

Half-a-dozen men lifted The Bishop by the front bumper.

The jack, carefully watched by Grampa, fell over while nothing was touching it. Stephen jiggled the spare wheel onto the axle. He reached for the bolts and, with Grampa's help, they were hand-screwed firmly in place.

"OK!"

The men lowered the car.

Nothing seemed to fall off or cause concern so a great cheer went up. Gideon gave his final help by grabbing the wheel spanner and tightening the bolts further. He was very keen and, having witnessed his strength in lifting the car, Stephen had to step in to stop him.

"No…no…! That's enough!" He took the spanner from Gideon, who wanted to keep going. "Any tighter and we'll never be able to undo them again. Thank you, thank you, very much!"

Grampa retrieved and folded up the jack. Stephen put away the tools. Yet again, Grannie and I hunted around for something to give the men who had helped. As I drove off towards the setting sun I couldn't help feeling that during this holiday we had received much more than we had given.

Still, the sun was setting and there were many miles to go. Foot down, we practically flew over the hills to reach Bridge Camp by nightfall.

Bridge Camp was situated on a cliff overlooking the Luangwa River. Our individual chalet rooms were set along a lamplit path. They were walled to hip-height, shaded by an enormous thatched roof and the gap in between was covered in netting – first chicken wire, then further thin-meshed mosquito prevention. I realised then that I had travelled far since first moving to Zambia. I ignored the rips and holes in the netting. I was oblivious to the spiders' webs adorning the thatch. I didn't object to the lack of wall and flimsy curtains that pretended to provide privacy. For us, for an overnight stay it was fine; although I would have loved to have given my parents-in-law more luxury than a walk to communal toilets – particularly when I discovered a fine-looking frog peering out though the overflow hole in the sink.

"One of these days we really must arrive somewhere on time," I said, recovering with a stiff drink.

Stephen turned to me and smiled. "Tomorrow we will. It's only three hours' drive."

"All right, that's likely to be before sunset, but next time … next time can we *please* get there on time?"

"Next time? Where are we going next?"

"Home, for my sister's wedding. Surely we can't mess up that journey?"

"We-ell…" Stephen threw back, then we both laughed.

I stretched and yawned. Africa was working her magic again. Our view was little more than a few bushes lit by our lamplight but the peace and quiet was overwhelming. All around we could hear nature unfolding itself: frogs belching, cicadas calling, hippos harrumphing in the river, the occasional bird crying to its mate in the dark. There was virtually no wind, just a gentle breeze rustling the leaves on the trees. Our lamplit world was in the middle of the wilderness, a safe citronella cocoon.

"The mozzie burner's close to going out," I said, nodding to the coil on my right.

"Must be time for bed," said Stephen, finishing his drink with a sigh. "It's been quite a day – indeed, quite a holiday."

"It certainly has," I said as I listened to the night-time sounds, then took a deep breath of the scented air. "It certainly has."

THE CHAIR

As the school term got into full swing, life resumed a steady routine. Grannie and Grampa were safely back home, with many a tale to tell at a dinner party, and Gwyn was enjoying her new job. After a couple of weeks Gwyn moved into her flat, containing little more than a bed and a few kitchen utensils. It was good to have the house to ourselves again after nearly two months with constant guests, although it was never short of people coming and going. Not only did we have Sherry and Precious for most of every day, but there was also our driver Justin. There were occasional hiccups with the transport arrangements, but I grew used to seeing him as I passed through the house. Gwyn still called round every morning for the journey to school with Matthew and often popped in later in the day as well.

My own employment was changing. After weeks of deliberation I had decided to leave EFZ, where I'd worked for the past year. For a few months I'd been helping a friend with some accountancy advice and it had become clear he needed more of my time and input in his company. And he would pay more, which ultimately swung the decision in his favour. My conscience wasn't clear about that, but I felt it was the right plan for my family, and me, in the long term.

I didn't know how to share my news with my colleagues at EFZ, other than to raise it at the end of our usual heads of department meeting following Tuesday morning devotions. At that point I blurted it out, a jumble of words showing my embarrassment. I looked at Joan, Fortune and Leah: people I loved so much, leaders in their community who worked so hard for their fellow Zambians. In so many ways I felt I was letting them down.

"I'll work my notice," I said, "so it won't be for a few weeks." I knew this would seem peculiar to them, since I'd observed most locals just left without saying anything. To give them their dues, when the main reason to move was an increase in pay, it usually overwhelmed the loss of a month's salary notice period. "And I'm not going until I find you a replacement," I added.

There was a moment's silence, then murmuring along the lines of, "Oh no!" and "Please don't go," and "We'll miss you." Their efforts to persuade me to stay were a little half-hearted. In all reality I knew they would prefer to have a Zambian in the role.

I spent the time advertising and interviewing. Given our experiences when employing a driver, I gave the candidates a little test, to see if they could actually do what they said they could do. A lot of people appeared to obtain qualifications and be able to talk profit and loss, debits and credits and other accountancy babble, but few were able to use the knowledge in practice. Certificates bought by wealthy parents? Possibly sometimes. It made me wonder if anywhere in the country was free from bribery and corruption.

I also wanted someone trustworthy and honest, as they'd be dealing with large sums of money that was given to support the poor in Zambia, not to supplement the employee's income. There was time for the replacement to start before I completed my three-month notice period. I was reasonably confident in him, though I left the organisation quietly and with a heavy heart. I'd always wanted the best for EFZ and perhaps – just perhaps – my departure was for the wrong reasons.

❧

"Gwyn's not back yet," I said as I chopped vegetables for dinner.

"Really?" Stephen was surprised. "Well, I'm glad she's making friends."

"Yes. It was lovely of Rachel to invite her for lunch after church this morning."

Stephen looked at his watch. "It's five o'clock – that's a long lunch." Then, after a thoughtful pause, "Should I call to make sure she's all right?"

I threw the onions into the frying pan. "Nah, she'll be fine."

Yet it was me, having put the kids to bed, who crept out for a walk around the compound, just to check. The Professor was still not back and no lights were on. I told myself not to worry: she was a responsible adult, she had her phone with her, it was not as if we didn't know the family she was visiting. But it was an awfully long lunch.

᷾

I had lost Matthew's shoes. Eleanor's face, hands and highchair were covered in cereal mush. My mug of tea had gone cold. I was in no mood for Monday morning.

"Morning!" Gwyn sang as she came in the front door.

"Hi there! How are you?"

"Fine!" She was glowing.

"Matthew, go and have a look under your bed," I said, while attempting to wipe Eleanor down, then turned to Gwyn. "Did you have a good time yesterday? You were back much later than expected." I put this as casually as I could, hiding the anxiety Stephen and I had shared the night before.

"Ooh yes! Mike and Rache are lovely! Mike's brother, Gareth, was there too. And… you know… we just chatted all afternoon, then watched a movie on the veranda in the evening."

"Sounds fun! Oh, morning Sherry! Do you know where Matthew's shoes are?"

Sherry paused on the threshold, then said, "Maybe his bedroom?" and promptly went to join Matthew in the hunt.

I finished with Eleanor and let her loose. She ran to give her Aunty Gwyn a big hug.

"Good job I cleaned her first," I laughed. Then, as Gwyn's comments gradually trickled through my Monday morning brain fog, I asked, "How did you watch a movie outside?"

"Gareth had a projector, so we could watch it on the wall. *Pirates of the Caribbean*. I've seen it before, but…"

Gwyn's eyes sparkled with delight. She'd had a great time.

"Excellent… excellent…" I said.

☙

Wednesday morning. Justin was in his usual seat, the plastic chair under the mulberry tree, reading a book.

I heard Gwyn's feet first, a kind of shlip-shlopping as she dragged them along the path. "Morning!" she called cheerily.

Justin replied, raising his hand in a brief greeting before returning to his book.

"Hi there! How are you this morning?" I asked as she came in through the door. "Did you get your marking done last night?" I was struggling to get a T-shirt over Matthew's head. After a sharp tug his head popped through, big grin across his face. I ruffled his hair and sighed: *I really ought to buy some bigger T-shirts.*

"Erm… no… At least, not all of it."

I lifted my head to look at her. She was peculiarly hesitant, and it was not like her to delay marking.

"Why not? Did you just mooch around?" I had to turn my face away from her. I hated the word 'mooch'. Gwyn used it all the time. I think I hated it most because I didn't have the time to mooch: children, job and life taking up every moment I had spare. I finished dressing Matthew.

"No. Well, kind of yes. Gareth brought a chair round, and we just chatted, and…" She petered off, before picking up again, "Well, by the time he left there wasn't a lot of time to do the marking."

"No, no… I guess not." I wondered at this visit. "A chair, you say?"

"Yes, I'd spoken on Sunday at Mike and Rachel's about how I didn't have any furniture and I really needed something to sit on."

"And now you have… a chair?"

"Yes. But only one: made the conversation a bit

difficult. I had to perch on the bed – you know, Matthew's old one, without the mattress."

I tugged at Matthew's shoes. "Right, boyo! All done!" I patted him on the head and picked up his lunchbox. "Let's go!"

Justin was roused from his book, The Bishop beeped as he unlocked the doors and I strapped Matthew into his car seat.

"Have a lovely day!" I gave him a kiss. "You too, Gwyn."

"I will!" She was beaming with joy as Justin started the car.

I waved goodbye as they reversed down the drive, Gwyn happily waving from the passenger seat and encouraging Matthew to do the same. As they left, I turned to go inside.

A chair! I said to myself, and shook my head with a smile.

☙

"OK, so you'll help?"

"Of course I will, Gwyn. What are your choices?" I asked.

"Skirt? Trousers?"

"Skirt."

"But the trousers go better with the smart top."

"Trousers, then. No – no, go and get them all. I'll judge best by seeing them. I'll refill your glass while you're gone."

"All right!" said Gwyn.

She left in a flurry, full of anxieties and excitement. I wandered through to the kitchen.

"Sorry love, you're on child duty this evening," I said to Stephen, who had already been assigned the duty of making dinner.

"Everything OK?"

"Oh yes. She doesn't know what to wear." Opening the fridge, I reached for the white wine.

"Doesn't know what to wear?" he repeated incredulously.

"That's right," I turned and grinned at him. "It's very important to know what to wear when you're not going on a date."

"So it isn't a date?" Stephen threw some carrots into the stir-fry.

"Oooh, no, no, no. They're going out for a drink, that's all. Friends."

"Ah. Friends." We laughed together and, as I poured the wine, I heard Gwyn call "Cooeee!" as she returned.

"Hi there! Wine's ready! Do you want to change in the spare room?"

"That'll be great."

Gwyn had make-up on: another first. I'm not sure that I had ever seen her dolled up like this before. Maybe at our wedding?

"Mu-um!" wailed Matthew.

"What is it love?"

"I'm hungry!"

"Daddy's just cooking dinner. It'll be ready in a couple of minutes."

"But I want *you* to cook dinner," said Matthew.

"Well, tonight Daddy's cooking. Mummy's got to help Aunty Gwyn for a few minutes. Why don't you go and wash your hands so you're ready?"

A rather grumpy little boy stomped across the living room and through to the bathroom, bumping unceremoniously into Gwyn as she emerged from the spare room.

"Oops – sorry Matthew!"

"Humph!" He stormed past her.

Gwyn looked at me quizzically.

"I'm not cooking dinner," I said and, as if that explained everything, Gwyn shrugged and asked what I thought.

"You look lovely!"

She did. It was a beautiful black dress.

"Isn't a bit too – well, you know – too… tarty?"

"Too short? Well, I doubt he'll think that."

"But do I want him to think that?"

"I don't know: what do you want him to think?"

No response. I was getting nothing out of her. "I'll try the trousers on," she said, and vanished. I put her wine on my dressing table and sipped at mine while waiting.

There was a tentative tap at the door before it was pushed open. "Well?" Gwyn's face was suffused with anxiety.

Again, she looked stunning. I told her so.

"I'm not sure about the shoes, though," she said.

"What you've got looks fine."

"Yes, but they'll kill me if I have to walk far."

"Ah – probably not the best option then. Personally, I'd go for comfort. There's nothing worse than having to hobble about because of your shoes."

"The alternative is…" There was a quick dash down the corridor and back again. "These!"

"Flip-flops?"

"Yep. That's all I've got. Or the brown ones with wedge heels."

I scratched my head. As flip-flops go these were smart: not the plastic you might buy at the seaside but a smart beaded frame with a pink silk flower at the junction between the toes. Nevertheless, the flip-flops really didn't go with the smart trouser outfit. Brown and black? Another no-no. Which left the blister-inducing black pumps, or…

"What size are you?" I asked.

"Size 4."

"Shame, can't lend you any of mine. You'd end up looking like a clown with over-sized feet!" It was a vain hope. Gwyn was smaller than me in all directions, so it was unlikely that any of my gear would ever flatter her. "OK, what about the pink shoes with the dress, but maybe with a pink wrap?"

"I don't have a pink wrap."

"Hmmm… there I may be able to help you."

I rooted around in my wardrobe and pulled out two options: pink with grey stripes, or a deep turquoise colour.

"Not sure about the grey," Gwyn said. She was right: it didn't enhance the outfit. "Does it really matter about the shoes?" she continued. "Does anyone really look at them?"

"Well, probably not. It depends if you are going to lift your legs up and wave them above the table."

"Only after too many Mosis!" she laughed.

"So – the trousers with flip-flops?"

"Yes," she said decisively. "But is this top right?"

I raised my eyebrows. Another problem? For a non-date this was a lot of worrying! "What's wrong with the one you've got on?"

"Well, is it too dull?"

It was a simple, black halter neck and, as with everything, it flattered her figure and drew attention to her beautiful face.

"No – definitely not too dull," I reassured her.

"But then I can't wear this necklace," she said, holding up a silver chain.

"Well, no, but I'm not sure that matters."

"And won't I be too hot in these trousers? Oh, really, I'd be better in the dress."

I sighed. I was not sure I was any help in this decision-making process. We'd come round full circle and she was in as much of a tizzy as she had been to begin with. I took a deep breath.

"In all honesty? I think either will be fine. He's not going to be interested in what you wear: he's interested in you. Wear what you'll be most comfortable in."

She smiled at me. "Yes, yes… you're right. I'll wear the…" She hesitated, looking at the options, then looked at me again. "I'll go and have my bath and decide after that."

It was all I could do not to bang my head against the wall in despair.

She bundled up her clothes and shoes, then dashed out of the house.

"Bye kiddees! Bye Stephen!"

"Bye-bye Aunty Gwyn!" they chorused.

I re-joined my family for dinner, now going cold.

"Is everything sorted?" Stephen asked. "Have you decided?"

"No – she'll decide after her bath. Truth is, I think Gareth would like her if she wore a hessian sack, but there you go!" I smiled at Stephen. "Don't forget – it's not a date!"

"Yeah right!" he said, eyes twinkling.

❧

Lying in bed that evening I asked him, "Do you remember when we first met?"

I liked teasing Stephen about this, because he didn't, although he grudgingly acknowledged my memory was probably correct.

"You know I don't," he said, turning a page of his book, "but I do remember our first date."

"Do you?"

"Yes – I took you out for dinner at Pierre Lapin."

"Really? I don't remember that."

He put his book down in mock horror.

"You don't remember?"

"Hey, hey, hey! At least I remember meeting you all those years before! And I do remember our first kiss."

He smiled. "Ah, yes. I remember that too."

We looked at each other, eyes twinkling.

"How about another one?" he said.

SCUTTLING ABOUT

I opened the cutlery drawer. There, bold as brass, was a beetle: less than an inch long and a reddish-brown colour. He (I assumed all bugs and beetles to be male until proven otherwise) took a moment to assess his new situation (on show, in broad daylight) and then vanished.

Africa had clearly taken full control of me, as I didn't scream. I barely let out a whimper. In fact, I was intrigued.

"What was that?" I asked the empty room, aware that I had heard scratching noises in the kitchen previously. Was this the explanation?

Frowning, I took a teaspoon to stir my hot chocolate then shut the drawer. I pottered through to the spare room and peered over Stephen's head at the laptop screen.

"Did you manage to connect?" I asked. I'd left him earlier cursing the inconsistencies of dial-up internet connection.

"Yes, eventually."

"Maybe affordable broadband will come to Zambia soon," I said, throwing in more optimism than I felt.

"We can dream," he said grumpily. "Still, I was able to email our parents and let them know we've arrived back safely."

"Good." I smiled and squeezed his shoulder. We'd only been away a week, an unmissable journey to the UK for my sister's wedding, but I could see he had a stream of work-related messages to plough through and could sense the tension rising. I watched him finish his latest response and, with a final flourish, hit the return button. I stood in silence, in mutual support, listening to the squeaky tune of the telephone line connection. The computer whirred round and seemed to be thinking hard about how it would send this tiny email. Seconds ticked by… then whoosh: it was gone. Vanished down the telephone line with more than a 50% chance of reaching its recipient.

Stephen rubbed his eyes. "Blimey – I can't believe how tired I am."

"Well, I don't suppose any of us slept very well on the plane last night."

"Yeah, but we all had a nap for a couple of hours before lunch. How can I still be tired?"

"It's what travel, and heat, and Africa, does to you," I said dismissively. "Six thousand miles? It's more than most people travel for a wedding. Still, I'm glad I did it. I'd have hated to have missed my sister's big day."

I had little to do for her wedding, as she was so organised and remarkably calm. I joined two of her best friends as a bridesmaid, recognising that I was not the tallest, nor the slimmest (by about twenty centimetres in each case) but at least I was the brownest. African sun had some merits.

I also had the honour of giving one of the Bible readings. I had practised it over the preceding days, trying to learn it by heart, but when it came to the crunch I had bottled out.

For expats, travelling home often became less of a holiday and more a round of visiting friends and family. While this was lovely, it wasn't the way I'd choose to spend all my precious time away from work, as it was draining and I needed some personal time to unwind. The expats I knew seemed to spend all their time trying to keep in touch with people, so when they eventually returned for good they wouldn't have dropped completely off the radar.

On that basis, the family wedding was a bonus, as I got to catch up with everyone in one fell swoop. My godmother had said that Eleanor was just like me at her age, though I couldn't imagine that myself. Eleanor was bright, cheery, happy, giggly and very interested in food. I know that as a toddler I had blonde curls, like she did, and that she'd inherited my blue eyes, but did I really like pink that much? Laugh so much? Flirt so much? I thought not.

My father had taken the news of our intention to extend our sojourn in Zambia very well. "I must plan another visit," he had said. I loved him for being non-judgemental of our proposals. Stephen had taken the opportunity while in the UK to put in the formal application for a six-month extension to his grant that would complete his research.

"Finished your tea?" I asked, holding out my hand for his mug.

"Almost," he said, reaching for the cooled liquid.

"I hope they find our missing suitcase," I said as he drank. "We never seem to travel without some sort of disaster. You done?"

Stephen passed his empty mug. "Could have been worse," he said, "and it may appear on the next flight in."

"I know." At least that suitcase hadn't included any of his work. "Have you much more to do?"

"Just need to answer these emails," he said.

I returned to the kitchen. As I filled a glass with filtered water, I saw something scamper across the counter and down the back of the cupboards, and sighed. *We're back in Africa with unidentified creatures scuttling around in the* dark, I thought. I switched off the light and closed the door firmly behind me, taking my water to the bathroom. Stephen was still at the computer in the next room.

"Matthew wasn't great this evening," I said as I squeezed some toothpaste onto my brush.

"Oh? Why do you say that?"

"I don't know. He was just out-of-sorts, grumpy, not his usual chirpy self. And then, after his bath, he snuggled up quickly for his bedtime storybook and went to bed with barely a murmur."

"He was probably exhausted from the flight, like the rest of us."

"I know, but–" I stopped, deciding to put aside my concerns. Stephen was probably right. We were all worn out from the travel, and Matthew had forced himself to stay awake very late on the plane. It wasn't helped by the copious amounts of chocolate available in his in-flight children's meal. Maybe the stimulating additives had finally caught up with him? I finished brushing my teeth, just about stopping myself from using tap water, and called to Stephen.

"Come on. Leave the computer. It'll still be there in the morning."

"I know. Just let me finish this and I'll be with you."

I was too tired to argue. He was already consumed by work issues and eager to return to his beloved research. I climbed into bed and, though I began flicking through a magazine, I was soon yawning and my heavy eyelids drooped closed.

&

"Where are the car keys?"

Monday morning at seven o'clock and the usual manic chaos before going to work had begun, made worse by it being the first day back. Our usual routines had easily been forgotten. The location of The Professor's keys was a mystery.

"I'm sure I left them here. Catharine, have you seen them?"

"Weren't they on the side, by the telephone?"

"No!"

"On top of the papers on the bench?"

There was a grunt, a rustling of paper, then an emphatic, "No!"

"Oh. No idea then, sorry."

Stephen growled in despair and dashed back to the study to pick up his things. I left Eleanor with a spoon and mushed up cereal, and avoided getting dollops of food flung at me by taking the used breakfast plates to the kitchen. I found Sherry already there, washing up the previous night's pans.

"Sorry – more plates," I said. She smiled in reply, dunking them in the water without question or complaint. I turned to put the kettle on for another mug of tea and, on opening the box where the teabags were kept, I found the keys.

"Stephen! They're here!"

He came rushing through.

"Oh, thank goodness! Where were they?"

"In with the teabags."

"Teab–?" He shook his head in disbelief. "Well, at least they're found. I'll start loading the car."

He picked up his rucksack and stuffed his laptop in amongst the papers. The first day back after a period away was always worrying: so much to catch up on, so much to do, so many potential disasters to rectify. To help keep the support of colleagues, there were gifts from the UK to distribute: shortbread, tea, make-up, as well as professional books and papers.

"Could you put my bags into The Bishop for me?" I asked.

"Of course. The keys are…?"

I took them from the wooden pot on the shelf, where they always lived.

"If you're OK, I'll go and wake Matthew. It's odd for him to have slept so long, but he was very tired last night."

"Sure, no problem."

The children's room was dark and Matthew still hadn't woken. The inseparable Teddy had become a pillow under his sleepy head, though the sheet and blanket had been flung off. Lying on his top bunk he held all the beauty and innocence of childhood in his peaceful face.

This all changed as I drew the curtain to let in light and gently called to him to wake. There were stretches and moans, a bleary eye opened to peer at me then, still heavy with sleep, closed. I could see the muscles extending in his face as he struggled in the battle for wakefulness.

"Come on, love. It's time to wake up. Eleanor's already having breakfast."

He looked at me groggily and crawled dutifully to the other end of the bed. I helped him down the ladder, out of love rather than necessity, and got a hot, sweaty hug for the privilege.

"Go on. Go to the bathroom then come through for breakfast."

He reluctantly peeled himself away from my embrace, shook off the last vestiges of sleep and walked away. Slowly, not the usual chirpy morning swagger, but compliant and quiet. I watched him go down the corridor, then I stepped through to the living room, at which point he started to cry.

Rushing back, I called softly, "Hey, you! What's wrong?"

He was standing on the bathmat in tears. I knelt down in front of him, looking into his tear-stained face and asked again. "What's wrong?" He flung himself at me and sobbed.

He was still hot. The cool morning air hadn't had much effect on the heat engendered by sleep. He was behaving so out-of-sorts that I was baffled. My boy was rarely ill. At three-and-a-half he'd barely had a cold to complain about. Panic rushed through me. If he had a fever could it be malaria?

I lifted him up in my arms and turned to the sink. Soaking a flannel in cold water I mopped his brow. Whether it was the comfort of mother or the shock of cold on his head I don't know, but the tears stopped.

"Feel better?"

There was an unconvincing nod.

"Let's go and find Daddy," I said. He was a paediatrician: he'd know what to do.

We found Stephen outside, loading the last of the boxes into the boot of the car. Seeing me with Matthew he came to say hello.

"Hey, what's up?" he said, noticing Matthew's miserable face. The tears started again, and he reached for his dad.

"I don't know," I answered on his behalf, "but he's

been teary and miserable since waking. And he's hot. Should I take him to get checked for malaria?"

My heart, full of worry, was thinking *yes, yes, yes*; my brain was wondering how to do that and get to work within the hour.

Stephen put Matthew down gently and looked at him at arm's length. "Maybe," he said. "Have you given him Calpol yet?"

"No, that was my next job."

"Start with that and see if the fever subsides." He smiled at his son, then, looking down, frowned. He leaned in closer to peer at his neck, pulling the pyjama top down a little.

"When did these appear?"

"What?" I said, bending down to look.

"These: the red spots."

Sure enough, around his neck and travelling up to his ears was an array of tiny red spots. In the darkness of the bedroom and the gloom of our bathroom and corridor I hadn't seen them. Only now, out in the morning sunshine, were they revealed.

"Let's take your top off, Matthew, and have a look."

Matthew lifted his arms feebly and let his father remove the pyjamas. There were a few more spread over his chest. Stephen pressed them gently, whitening the skin. He lifted his boy up again, ruffling his hair with his hands.

"I think, dear boy, you may have chicken pox."

༄

The radio blared out the World Service news, eventually rousing Stephen enough to switch off the beeping alarm that accompanied it. He lay there momentarily with his hand resting on the white box, then turned his sleep-filled body around and rubbed his eyes. He looked, started, rubbed his eyes again and said, "Hello! What are you doing here?"

If looks could kill, I'm sure mine would have done at that moment. He had slept through the night. I knew: I'd watched him. His shock now was on finding his son in bed next to him. Matthew had been there since one o'clock in the morning, when he'd woken for the third time, crying because his spots were sore. I had been none too happy at getting up repeatedly to comfort a boy who was scratching his chicken pox, so after a discussion with Stephen, he'd suggested that Matthew sleep with us.

"That way," Stephen had said, "we can keep an eye on him, try to stop him scratching."

Stephen, of course, had simply rolled over and gone back to sleep. I had pursed my lips and wearily plodded through to Matthew's room, gently coaxing my boy to come. Any moment of wakefulness during the night made him reach to scratch some part of his body. I'd held onto his hands, stroked his hair and whispered in his ear. For five hours he had slept fitfully: waking, crying, scratching, being held and soothed by his mother.

As dawn broke, I was worn ragged but my son, despite the alarm, was finally dozing. I did not take Stephen's surprise well. In fact, I took it so badly that for a long time I was speechless. Eventually I said through gritted teeth, "You told me to bring him into our bed."

I didn't add, "*then you fell asleep, took up your half of the bed while I shared mine with a wriggly, scratchy, feverish child and look! I'm nearly falling off this end, and my share of the blankets is at best mediocre.*" It seemed mean.

"How's he doing?" Stephen softly asked.

"You mean other than being awake most of the night? Oh, fine."

Stephen looked at me, opened his mouth to speak, then wisely shut it again. Looking down at his son, he stroked Matthew's head, then asked me, "Would you like a cup of tea?"

Why, oh why, did that do it? All my anger and resentment dissipated. Five minutes later we were sitting in bed, Matthew positioned more centrally between us. With a steaming mug of tea in hand I had a much calmer disposition.

"I hope he's better tonight," I said, "because I'm not sure I can do that again."

"I'll put calamine lotion on the spots before I head for work," Stephen said. "It's what – day three now? It shouldn't last much longer. Is he still getting new spots?"

"Hard to tell: his stomach and chest are covered in them, most now blistered, scabby or weeping." I gazed at my beautiful boy, his face splattered with the red pustules. My heart hurt for him, willing him to get past the illness and praying he'd escape unscarred.

Stephen looked at me. "He'll be fine," he said gently, activating the doctor's bedside-manner he used to calm frantic mothers. I knew he was right, but somehow my emotions were screwed up inside, rational thinking and heartache fighting a pitched battle.

"He was so ill yesterday. I came home from work to find him on Sherry's back. He's nearly four, and some weight! Yet she was calmly carrying him round in her chitenge, and he was in no mood to protest." *More than that*, I thought: *he was quite content.* I'd have said he was loving it, if it wasn't that he'd had such a long, miserable face and he'd been unable to do anything but flop.

We sipped our tea in silence.

"No sound from Eleanor yet this morning," I commented.

"How's she been?" Stephen asked.

"Fine," I began, but then realised the thought behind his question. Matthew had chicken pox: how long until she got it? I was worried about my toddler; how much more would I worry about Eleanor? "What's the incubation period?"

"A couple of weeks."

"Eleanor's got no symptoms now, so presumably she didn't catch it at the same time as Matthew. So we can expect her to come down with it at – what? The end of next week?"

"Maybe. And of course she may not get it at all."

"Is it a problem at her age? She's only just two."

Stephen shook his head. "No, not particularly. It's just worst for adults."

I took a big slurp of tea and offered up yet more prayer. Much of me didn't want Eleanor to get this at all – the last thing I needed was another week of sleepless nights and frantic worry about fevers. On the other hand, it was a disease best had in childhood. Once children have had it they are usually immune from getting it again.

Even in his sleep Matthew was scratching. I reached to hold his hand. My world focused back in to this point, this moment, these spots. For all my knowledge that most children got chicken pox, it remained painful to watch my son battle the itch.

෴

Over the year that we had been attending our church it had grown considerably. Instead of meeting fortnightly, the services were now weekly. This meant twice as much work to organise it, but double the opportunity to try out different cakes with tea afterwards. We no longer met in one member's house, enjoying the comfort of her squishy, living-room sofas, but instead gathered in the music room of Gwyn's primary school. Matthew was now back at the attached pre-school with his friends. They all seemed to have escaped the chicken pox, though he did pass it on to his sister. Eleanor would be joining him at pre-school in the New Year, as she'd now attained the grand age of two. The Bishop was getting very used to the journey to and from this group of buildings.

Only in an African church, though, would a particular school project brought by a primary school girl fascinate everybody so much. After the service she proudly showed her excellent work, propping it up behind the cake table (a particularly tasty array that day due to the presence of 'stroopwaffeln' from our Dutch members). The display boards were opened to reveal a detailed description of cockroaches. Perhaps as many as twenty varieties were shown, for the most part with (dead) examples pinned to the board. They varied in size, colour and general fearsomeness.

In the car on the way home I spoke with Stephen about the cockroaches.

"Wasn't it an amazing piece of work?" I said. "She'd set it out so well. All the biology, and the names of the different species."

"Yes," Stephen said thoughtfully. "Yes."

Silence.

"Are you thinking what I'm thinking?"

I glanced at Stephen. "Probably."

"That our kitchen is infested with cockroaches?"

"Yep!"

"All through the cutlery drawer?"

"Yep!"

Eurgh!

"Shall we go home via Game and get some poison?"

"Yes please!"

CHRISTMAS AND NEW YEAR

Christmas loomed. After the frenetic end-of-term activities, we decided to indulge ourselves with Christmas lunch at a hotel about an hour's drive from Lusaka, plus an overnight stay to sleep off our excesses. Stephen and I had the most romantic idyll: a big four-poster bed, crisp white sheets and a ceiling fan whirring quietly above. It was a shame that we had to have our two children with us as well.

Our treat started by relaxing with a gin and tonic in the shade of a tree in the hotel grounds. Gwyn joined us for this and lunch, with the intention of driving The Professor back home mid-afternoon for a second Christmas dinner with Gareth and his family. There's dedication to a relationship. Together, we shared in the excitement of Christmas presents and young children. Matthew had had plenty of practice with his birthday just a few days earlier, and he was very keen to help everyone with their unwrapping.

"All right! Who's going first?" Stephen asked.

"Me! Me! Me!" shouted Matthew, jumping up and down with his hand in the air.

"Well, what have we got here… is this one for you?" Stephen took a parcel from the bag and passed it to his son. "And, of course, one for you too, Eleanor."

Eleanor took her gift and shook it before handing it to Gwyn.

"Would you like help opening it?" Gwyn asked, to a series of furious nods. Matthew was already making headway ripping off his paper.

"Thomas!" he exclaimed, holding up the train. His face shone with the delight of surprise. Given his current train obsession, Thomas the Tank Engine could hardly fail. Matthew had been responsible for naming our tortoises earlier in the year so now one of them was called ThomasTheTankEngine (Thomas, for short). It took all our efforts to persuade him not to give the other one the same name, but in the end Matthew settled for Tom Fum.

There were further rounds of gifts: books from family in the UK, toys and sweets from Aunty Gwyn. The joy on the children's faces was more than enough to please me for a year.

"And this one is yours," said Stephen, handing over a box-shaped present, a little bigger than A4 size.

"For me? Wow!" I was delighted and wondered what it could be. Presumably he had picked up something when in the UK for a week in November. It felt like a very heavy book, but I couldn't imagine what hardback was worth his investment. A dictionary, maybe?

Matthew was eager to help. If it were possible to get prizes for speed of unwrapping he'd probably have won. At his birthday party he'd opened all the gifts from his friends without me noticing, so I was completely unable to attribute each gift to the giver. It made thank you letters a lot more complicated.

"Thank you Matthew. How about you slide your finger along there…" I indicated the edge of the paper. He tried to slide between the paper sheets, but hit a snippet of sellotape; so then he abandoned caution and ripped the lot.

"Oh, all right. We won't bother to re-use this paper then!"

Inside was a white plastic bag, and in that a bubble-wrap envelope.

"What on earth do you think it is Matthew?"

"A train?" he asked, hopefully.

"Well, no, I don't think Daddy's bought Mummy a train. It's a – oh!"

I was rendered speechless. A laptop computer!

"Stephen! I… When…? Why…? I don't need this!"

He shrugged, delighted by my surprise. "I thought you could do to venture into the world of Apple Macs."

"But I've already got a laptop!"

"I know, but it's becoming old and slow. Perhaps the children will use it."

"Oh, Catharine – your face is a picture!" Gwyn clapped her hands and laughed with glee. "I've never seen anyone so gobsmacked!"

I closed my mouth, thinking it was in danger of becoming a permanent 'O' shape, then grinned broadly. "Thank you!" I said to Stephen, hoping the love and gratitude in my eyes outweighed the shock and horror that my gift to him was so pathetic in comparison.

Having opened all our presents and let the children run off around the trees I suggested that, in the few moments we had before lunch, Stephen took the suitcase from the car and put it in our room.

Stephen looked at me blankly.

"Is that OK?" I was confused by his silence.

"Ye-es. But I don't know where our suitcase is."

It was my turn to look blank. "But it's in the car – isn't it?"

"I just don't remember seeing it when I took the presents out. Worse than that, I'm sure the car is empty."

Gwyn was watching us like a tennis match. "Better go check!" she said brightly. "It's OK – I'll entertain the children here. You'll only be a couple of minutes – right?"

"Yeah, back in a mo!"

Stephen and I crossed the grass in silence and went through the reception area back to The Bishop, with a gnawing feeling that things weren't going to go according to plan.

The Bishop was filthy, covered in a layer of orange dust from our drive up to the lodge. I was in my Sunday best (it was Christmas Day, after all) so left Stephen to manhandle the rear door. After our various off-road travelling exploits it was stiff to open and I wanted to avoid covering my summery, white dress with a dusting of fine terracotta powder.

Sure enough, Stephen was right: the car was empty, save for a few sweet wrappers and one of Eleanor's books that had fallen down the side. No sign of the suitcase.

I knew who to blame. "You didn't pick it up from the corridor?"

"I thought you'd put it in the car. You were packing all the other stuff."

"I was sorting out the children. I–" I stopped. Arguing was pointless. "What do we do now? Shall I go home and get it?"

"But that would mean missing lunch. You can't do that, not on Christmas Day."

We were in a complete quandary. We didn't have the fuel to do the journey home and back, and being Christmas Day there weren't any garages open. We had the choice of forfeiting our luxury night away, or making do. This upmarket hotel was not going to be impressed by the state of its guests, with no change of clothes (although the children had just received new T-shirts from Grannie, which was a blessing) and no toiletries.

"Well, I guess none of our teeth will fall out if we don't clean them for twenty-four hours," I said. "Sure, we'll have bad breath, but perhaps we can steal some mints from the dinner table?" What a ridiculous situation we'd got ourselves into. I couldn't help but giggle, releasing the tension.

"My only problem might be insulin." There was a pause while Stephen checked what he had in his pen and thought this through. Eventually he concluded, "I think I'll be fine – just might need to watch what I eat for breakfast."

"You sure?"

"Yes," he nodded and grinned. "Lunch?"

We had a sumptuous feast: a vast array of salads, soup and starters, followed by a buffet choice of meats (and a vegetarian option for me), then a table laden with choices of dessert. Stephen had tried chilli crocodile tails ("Why not?" he said); I had sampled as many of the puddings as I could. Bloated, but happy, we beached our bodies in the reclining chairs by the pool.

Mid-afternoon, Gwyn found enough energy to move and left us to go back into town, though the prospect of an evening with Gareth was more motivation than the prospect of more food. The children splashed around happily in the shallow area of the pool and, shaded by a tree, I had the chance to read my book. A hot Christmas still felt strange, though we were grateful that the rainy season had decided to hold off for another day.

What made me look up when I did, I'll never know.

"Stephen!" I screamed.

He'd seen her too. Somehow Eleanor had slipped in the water. She was thrashing and floundering about, trying to get up, trying to get air. I was watching my daughter drown.

I followed every step in slow motion as Stephen ran over, jumped in and lifted her high out of the water. She coughed and spluttered, and cried. Running over, I grabbed a towel and took her from my husband, cradling her close.

"Don't do that!" I whispered to her as we rocked together, both trying to calm down. "Don't do that again."

I cried, holding her tight until the wailing had subsided and she was wriggling to get down. Meanwhile Stephen stood beside us both, dripping wet in the only clothes he had for our entire break.

❧

My sister's wedding in October had cheated us of two events. The first was that on the one day we took Matthew out of pre-school, KK (Kenneth Kaunda, the first President of Zambia) had visited to celebrate forty years of Independence. The other was our church's camping weekend away. We could do nothing about the former except look at Gwyn's photographs, but for the latter, having heard such good reviews, we could. We decided to book ourselves into the same campsite for a few days over New Year.

The prospect of camping was an area of marital discord, as Stephen hankered after it for the adventure and I liked my warm, dry, comfortable bed. Here was a fair compromise. We stayed in a pre-erected safari tent on site. There was a lovely wooden veranda with a view over the lake, and inside there was sufficient room for four single beds, a wardrobe and chest of drawers. At the back of the tent was an en suite shower room (with hot, flowing water). Plenty of room to move around, lots of head-height and little fear of the contraption collapsing in a gust of wind: the perfect tent. Even all our food was cooked for us, in the main area of the lodge a short walk away.

There was no particular reason for our visit other than to escape for a few days. Most of our expat friends had gone to their home countries for the Christmas holidays, and even the locals seemed to have left town. Here was peace and quiet: the countryside that city-dwellers long for. The game park had a few antelope (one particularly fine-looking Tsessebe), giraffes and then some smaller wildlife. Allegedly the lake was free from crocodiles, which made us happy to go canoeing but I still wasn't prepared to risk swimming. On reflection, that was a ridiculous way to exercise my fear, since the greatest risk is at the edge of the water with crocodiles sliding up to snap at ankles. Getting into a boat at the water's edge was probably as risky as swimming.

The owners of the campsite had invited us to their New Year's Eve party, encouraged to dress as something beginning with N. Not having anticipated a fancy dress party, and having a complete blank on ideas for anything that began with N (apart from 'nothing' or 'nude', neither of which I was prepared to contemplate, or 'nappies', which wasn't much better) we decided to be party-poopers and have a normal night's sleep. I couldn't remember the last time I had missed seeing in the New Year, but by 8.30 p.m. all four of us were in bed and out for the count.

By two in the morning, that had changed. Eleanor had woken and was chattering away about nothing in particular and it was irritating me no end. I tried gentle persuasion from the warmth and comfort of my bed.

"Eleanor – shush love! Lie down and go back to sleep."

For a few seconds this had silenced her, but then the babble began again. I rolled over, to try to ignore the noise and fall back asleep. Eleanor's middle-of-the-night chirpiness was not to be ignored. Perhaps it is simply the mother-radar that cannot be switched off, but there was no way I was going to sleep until she stopped.

I gazed at the canvas above me. Not a grand double bed, as at Christmas, but two singles, and mattresses on the floor for the children. Not a fan whirring overhead, but the sound of the bush all around, draughts eking their way through gaps in the tent.

And my wretched girl still babbling away in a language of her own.

Reluctantly I dragged myself out of my bed and across to Eleanor's.

"Ellie – you've got to lie down and go to sleep."

She stared at me unseeingly. I wasn't sure she realised she was awake and making a noise. "Come on, love, lie down."

Biddable as ever, with a bit of gentle pressure from me she lay down. I moved her books to the end of the bed, replaced the blankets neatly over her and gave her a kiss.

"Mum? What's going on?"

Now Matthew was awake. "Sshh, boyo, everything's fine," I told him. "Eleanor's just going back to sleep."

I leaned over and give him a kiss too, then retreated to my bed. I was wondering if I might actually fall asleep this time when Eleanor started up again.

Matthew said firmly, "Eleanor, be quiet!"

That made me smirk: he sounded so like me! I braced myself for my next trip out of bed, knowing I had no ability to cope with a major sibling argument at three o'clock in the morning.

But, remarkably, his strict tone seemed to work – at least, for a short while. I relaxed back into the pillow. *Happy New Year, Catharine.* I wondered what the year would bring. Stephen had received confirmation of an extra six months' funding in the week before Christmas. Now it was settled: instead of returning to the UK in July, at the completion of the original two years, we would still be in Zambia this time next year. *We could come back to this campsite for New Year again,* I thought, then immediately dropped that idea when I realised I'd have to plan fancy dress outfits. *Another six months? Perhaps I could extend my work contract, maybe apply for a more permanent visa?* I wondered what the current rules and regulations were for that. It had been such a fabulous year and I could now make concrete plans for staying longer. Little did I know then that a further step in that direction would come within a couple of weeks.

The silence hadn't lasted. In the dim light I could see that Eleanor was sitting up again, turning pages of her books. I was trying the option of ignoring her. Unfortunately, her brother couldn't.

"Mu-um! Can you make Eleanor shut up?" Matthew complained.

I groaned and lost my temper.

"Eleanor!" I shouted at her. "I've told you already. Be quiet and go to sleep."

"What's going on?" Finally Eleanor's shenanigans had filtered into Stephen's slumbering brain and we were all awake. I told him Eleanor had been sitting on her bed, chatting, for ages and she wouldn't just lie down and go to sleep.

"Oh, is that all?" he grunted, turning over, and (to

placate me) called out, "Eleanor, do go to sleep."

She stopped what she was doing and lay down. The silence lasted and, an hour or so later, even I joined her in the land of nod.

Sunlight woke us at 6 a.m., as usual. At breakfast we looked far worse for wear than the revellers who had stayed up all night, dressed as Nurses and Nuns.

BEWARE THE FALLING AVOCADOS

I'd pretty much lost interest in small talk, or talk about small people. It was the fifth children's birthday party I'd attended in eight days, a quick calculation showing that April was a fecund month. My children, of course, loved all these parties and the chance to run around madly, jumping on bouncy castles and sliding into paddling pools. Though I enjoyed the hospitality (tea and cake have never been a problem for me), I found myself waiting for a suitable moment to leave. Returning from the toilet (a trip I'd taken to kill time) I bumped into Sara hobbling along the terrace. Mother to one of Matthew's friends, Sara worked as an accountant so we usually chatted about financial computer packages, Zambian tax and other matters that risked boring everyone else. She once suggested that I should keep my money in the freezer, the reasons for which now evade me.

"What's happened to you?" I asked, offering to take her plate and glass while she found somewhere to sit.

"I'm fine," she replied. "I just stubbed my toe badly opening the wardrobe this morning. Painful, but not life-threatening."

"Ouch! I'm sorry about that," I said, hurriedly adding, "Sorry for the pain, that is, rather than the lack of threat to life…"

She laughed my blunder off. "Everything seems to be falling apart at the moment," she said. "I'm having problems with my teeth, one of which added crunch to my sandwich yesterday. And my elbow has been stiff and aching for the last few weeks – reasons unknown."

"Crikey! You really are in the wars. Have you had yourself checked out by the doctor?"

"Yes, I'm on antibiotics and anti-inflammatories and I've an appointment with the dentist next week." She took a sip of her wine. "I think it's like being married for a long time. When you get married, you have a wedding list and fill your house with new equipment and furniture – all warrantied and in perfect working order. Then, ten… fifteen… twenty years on things begin to break down and all of a sudden you have to fix them or replace the lot. This is what's happening with my body."

"It's not that bad, surely!" I exclaimed.

"You're very kind," she said, "but I've reached the stage of life when all that used to work perfectly is showing its age and needs to be replaced or repaired. Passing the big Four-O is clearly detrimental to health."

My laughter was only tempered by the terror that it wasn't that far off for me either.

"Work taking a backseat for a while, then?" I teased.

I knew her well enough to recognise that wouldn't be the case. She'd only be avoiding work if there were fears about work permits. All expats lived under the same threatening shadow in this regard. However tightly we stuck to the government rules, and however assiduous we were at ensuring we were compliant with the regulations, and however much paperwork we had stamped in triplicate and signed by the Queen herself, still we worried that a grumpy official would call by, declare us to be working illegally and throw us out of the country. Given that would be preceded by a period in jail, and I can't imagine that a Zambian cell would be much fun, we were paranoid about getting things right.

"Actually," she said, in an uncharacteristic drawn out fashion and looking to the sky for inspiration, "actually, we're moving."

I gasped. "Moving? Where to?"

"Back to South Africa."

I was open-mouthed with astonishment, then upset for Matthew who loved his little buddy so very much.

"Why are you going? When are you going? What–? Oh, I have hundreds of questions. Start with the why!" I stammered to a stop.

"My husband's work. It seems more sensible to do it from South Africa. Here, they aren't being helpful in renewing his work permit so…" She shrugged her shoulders. "Most of his work can be done from Jo'burg, with the occasional trip north. I'll get a better job back home too, so away we go. It'll probably be at the end of next month."

"Next month! That's not giving you much time."

"It'll be enough," she said. I decided to take mental notes, for one day I might have to do this myself. Not part of our current plans, I knew, but nothing was certain.

Then my brain went into expat mode: if someone

was leaving, did they have anything I wanted?

And my brain's immediate response was: *Yes. I want their house.*

We had now been in Zambia over eighteen months, living in a semi-detached bungalow. I had grown used to its shady garden, the scratchy grass that tried to force its way out of the orange earth beneath the massive mulberry tree, the bars outside every window and even the highly polished brown concrete floor. Our house had become home. Gradually we had filled it with furniture and had adapted the layout to suit our needs, compensating for the tiny kitchen and the lack of curtains at most windows.

But Sara's house was different. It was spacious, detached and, most significantly, it was directly opposite the main school gates. I'd be able to walk the children to pre-school! What a bonus! In time we would outgrow the bungalow and, if we had to move, surely we should move to the best there was?

My thoughts were interrupted by the arrival of the birthday cake (large, fuchsia pink and with a Barbie doll stuck in the middle) and the obligatory singing of, "Happy Birthday to you". The local custom had a second verse, "How old are you now?" then, chanted loudly, "Are you one? Are you two? Are you three?"

This tended to work less well with adults.

The scramble to surround the cake separated me from Sara and I didn't get another chance to talk to her before we all parted. At the end, on handing out the traditional party bag, the birthday girl's mother gave every child one extra. The second bag was clear plastic, half-full of water and contained two fish.

"I was trying to think of something different for the party bag, not the usual plastic gifts," she explained. We all nodded, knowing how difficult it was to come up with (and source) something interesting as a gift.

Besides, I'd already received four other pieces of tat that week. "You just need a bowl and a bit of greenery," she went on, "and they last forever."

I was far too polite to do anything other than open and shut my mouth like the guppies I held. I told Matthew to say thank you before we hastily made our exit.

Just a bowl and some greenery? I thought. *How on earth is this going to work?*

❧

I arrived home motivated by two urgent matters: securing a house, and buying appropriate paraphernalia for guppy survival. Short term, the guppies were put in the kitchen mixing bowl and left to fend for themselves, since I couldn't improve their lives much before the shops opened on Monday morning.

The house, though, was more pressing. As soon as it was common knowledge that Sara was leaving others would be clamouring for the property. I had to act quickly: agree it with my friend, check the rental and secure it with her landlord. But the first hurdle was the most demanding: negotiation with Stephen. I chose to find some neutral territory.

"Let's go for a cake at the showgrounds," I said. "My treat."

"Yey!" screamed Matthew, who had little need of this after two hours of high-sugar-content birthday party, while Eleanor jumped up and down in delight. Their enthusiasm, and the prospect of a decent coffee, secured my husband's attendance. Bribery: such a powerful tool.

Our destination was the café that operated out of a small booth in a garden near the entrance to the Agricultural Showgrounds. Once a year, at the beginning of August, the showgrounds were the home of the Agricultural Show, a magnificent spectacle of animals, produce and business from around the country. I would make a beeline for the red, green and blue baby chicks, which delighted me every time. The colours came because the eggs were injected with food dye, much like my dad's experiments with snowdrops and coloured ink. I'm not sure how ethically sound the practice was, but I was reassured that the colours just faded as the chicks grew older. For the other fifty-one weeks of the year the buildings on the site were rented out to businesses, which the café neatly served.

The approach to the showgrounds was down a long straight road past the polo grounds.

"Horses!" Matthew exclaimed as we passed the stables.

"Aren't they beautiful," I said. Their glossy coats shone in the afternoon sun. Undoubtedly those horses were treated well.

"Horses have necks," said Matthew. This was a slightly unexpected observation, but indisputable.

"So they do, Matthew," said Stephen. "So they do."

"But shorter than a giraffe's," he added.

"Yes, yes…" Again, neither of us could quibble with his factual accuracy.

"Everything has a neck," said Stephen.

That was his downfall.

"No they don't Daddy. Walls don't have necks. Cars don't have necks."

"Well, no Matthew, but…"

"Trees don't have necks. Wheels don't have necks."

"No…"

"Chairs don't have necks. Grass doesn't have a neck."

"Matthew!"

"Stairs don't have necks."

"MATTHEW!" Stephen finally made Matthew stop. "Matthew: I'm wrong, you're right. Not everything has a neck."

I grinned sneakily. My son had turned four years old and had managed to get one over his father, a rare event for anyone. I couldn't wait for him to have many more opportunities.

Walking from the car park to the café, we passed under an avocado tree. It was huge, towering above us all and shading a small pond in the garden. The owners had thoughtfully pinned a sign on its trunk: *Beware the falling avocados*. Stepping over the splattered fruit remains on the path, I had little doubt they could kill.

Our children ran round the gardens, excited by the small climbing frame and swing. Settling down with our drinks, I began by telling Stephen Sara's news. I stirred the spoon around my mug and braced myself.

"It means their house will be up for rent." Gulp. "You know where it is, right? I was wondering if we should consider taking it."

Silence, except for some birds in the tree and Eleanor squealing behind me. "So *that's* the reason for this," he said ponderously, rubbing his chin.

I hung my head guiltily. "It's a great size," I began my justification. "A long driveway and a big garden. I poked my head in the living room and that's enormous." I petered out.

"What we've got now is just fine. Why do we need to move?" he argued.

"It's opposite the school," I finished lamely, despite that being a principal reason to move. "We'll save a fortune in fuel."

Perhaps I simply had itchy feet. We hadn't moved house for over eighteen months, which was practically a record since we'd been married. For me, this was us planning for a future in Zambia: a long term family home. I wanted our own independence, rather than being reliant on our landlord and his employees. I wanted a little distance from Gwyn.

I wasn't sure how to tell her brother that.

"It's a lot bigger," I carried on. "There must be enough bedrooms and, as the children grow, the space will be invaluable. They can't share a bedroom for ever."

"Neither of them is five yet! We've got a few more years before that's necessary."

"Maybe."

"And won't it cost more? Prices are rising, you know."

This was not a spurious concern. Rent in Lusaka had been rising astronomically, comparable to rents back home in the UK. I often looked in the window of the estate agents at Manda Hill and wondered how on earth anyone was paying for the houses. Local friends blamed the expats funded by large multi-nationals who wanted their employees to be happy and comfortable living in a foreign land.

"I know it'll be more expensive, but we can afford a little more than we're paying at present. And we can make a judgement on that when we know the exact amount. If it's too much, then it's obviously no," I said.

I watched Stephen's face as he thought everything through. Had I found a chink in his armour?

At that point, Matthew returned, all hot and bothered from running around. He'd already removed his T-shirt and curtailed adult conversation as he gulped down his bottle of fizzy orange and stripped off the remainder of his clothes to run back and play. Eleanor (thankfully fully dressed) worshipped her big brother and toddled after him, peppering the air with delighted shrieks.

I turned back to Stephen. "Maybe we should get these two home," he said.

"I know," I said reluctantly. "It's going to take ages to calm them down before bed."

As we finished our drinks and tidied up the mess our children had made, I put in a final comment. "Look, the house may be totally wrong for us, but we could at least have a look at it. There's no harm in that."

He took a deep breath. "OK then: give Sara a ring. But I'm not promising anything," he added, with a stern look.

"Thank you," I practically whispered.

It has not been often in life that I have really known what I wanted, but this was one of those occasions. The last time we'd chosen to move (rather than being forced into it by emigrating) we'd bought a bigger house in London. I had been nine months' pregnant: Eleanor's arrival coincided with the agreement of our purchase offer. This time I couldn't blame the nesting instinct: this time it was just a deep knowledge that this house would be right for us. I rang Sara without delay, and the next day she gave us a guided tour.

It was more than I could have asked for: five bedrooms, a huge open living/dining area and a kitchen that had more floor space than many houses back in the UK. Of course, this house was in Zambia so not without its quirks. The cooker had gaffer tape holding it together, and there was an ominous bulge in one of the kitchen ceiling panels but, in comparison with our current house, it felt like a palace. We'd have an en suite bathroom and it looked like all the taps matched, and the sanitary ware was white rather than an ageing yellow. Behind the house were a swimming pool and a tennis court (how ridiculous was that, to live in a house with a tennis court?) and at the end of the plot was a very serviceable servants' quarters.

It was lovely. It would work for us, I knew it.

❧

The guppies' mixing bowl home could not last and I made a rushed trip to the pet shop on Cairo Road. I was clearly not the first to visit, since he greeted me with, "Oh, from the party!" Within no time at all I had been sold a fish tank, pump, food and other fishy paraphernalia.

Back home I was then tasked with assembling it and transferring the fish. I was about to tip the fish straight into the tank full of clean water when Stephen stopped me. It turned out that he was something of an authority on fish care, in that he knew something whereas I knew nothing.

"You can't do that!" he said. "The tricky bit is moving them. They don't like a change of water."

"Even though you have to do that on a regular basis?"

"Yep, despite that. You have to keep the water at the same temperature and get them accustomed to it slowly."

"Or…?"

"Or they die," he said flatly.

I was none too keen on our new additions, but I held no criminal intent as a fish murderer. With some trepidation I mixed the waters, gradually emptying the mixing bowl contents into the newly constructed fish heaven. A gravelly bottom, a selection of green plants and even a tacky plastic stone cave adorned the tank. The water bubbled gently as air flowed from the pump. How much happier could a guppy fish be?

❧

By the end of the week Stephen had agreed a rental with Sara's landlord and I was ecstatic. Having decided everything in principle, it was a further three months until we moved. Foolishly, I had mentioned my fish tank investment at the school gate. The next day I had a further four fish swimming around the tank. From being a pet-free home a year earlier I now had to plan a move for twelve: the four of us, two tortoises and six guppies.

It might have been less than two years since we had moved country, but I had forgotten how stressful moving house was. All my spare time was filled as I rushed around town to ensure no-one cut off the electricity and confirmed that the phone line wouldn't alter and informed organisations of a change of address and wondered how one organised the water supply.

It was nerve-wracking telling Gwyn. I wasn't sure how she would take it, as we abandoned her to live 'on her own' on the old complex. It also meant that we didn't need to employ Justin any more for moving the kids to and from school. But as with the decision to move, this all fell into place. A school house became available for Gwyn and (ironically) she soon moved to live near us. And Justin wanted to set up his own church and organisation, so he left quite contentedly.

One saving, but another three to be employed. Our next challenge was the employment of guards and gardeners to work on the plot.

WE EAT TORTOISES

The new house had about an acre of land which Stephen and I had no hope of gardening by ourselves. The combination of that and a need for overnight security cover meant employing three new members of staff. The house was surrounded by ten-foot high walls with barbed wire across the top, yet it was the social norm to employ guards. Stories were rife of attempted, and successful, burglaries, as thieves climbed over the most protected walls and broke in through any window without bars. The strong levels of security were one of the first things we had noticed as different from the UK when we arrived nearly two years earlier, and yet I never felt unsafe. Maybe the security worked? Nevertheless, we decided to employ an overnight guard and a couple of gardeners (one of whom would work a guard night-shift during the week). With this, there would always be a presence on the plot, the garden would be watered, the gate would be answered and we could sleep at ease.

Finding new staff was never straightforward, as we had noted in our efforts with employing a driver about six months earlier. I started by enquiring at work, asking the gardener-cum-gatekeeper if he knew of anyone. He looked thoughtful and said, "Yes, Madam," then scurried off.

This was difficult to interpret. "Yes, Madam" was the usual response to any question or statement and didn't necessarily reflect any comprehension of the issue at hand. The slightly mystified gaze up to the sky weakened my faith in him, but the rush to leave was more hopeful. Most of all, I knew that finding a job for someone else could be lucrative for the agent. If it was a good job and well paid, then at the very least the new employee was in the other's debt; my suspicion was that they often got some financial reward as well.

A few hours later I was presented with his suggestion: his son. Henry was a skinny nineteen-year-old who shuffled nervously into my office. Eye contact was almost non-existent and his response to my questions was mainly "Yes, Madam", so my confidence was already on the wane. But I knew his father was a good, honest and reliable worker, and I saw no major problems with the state of the garden around the office, so decided I should trust him. He was the first to be employed.

"He'll be fine!" I said to Stephen, when he expressed his doubts later that evening. "He's young, but we can give him a job, a start in life."

"Hmmm," he said non-committally. "Well, hopefully Calvin will be able to teach him a thing or two."

Calvin had been recommended by the gardener Sara had employed on the plot. He'd been spoken of as 'his brother', which we'd loosely interpreted as some distant relation or maybe a friend who lived nearby, until he appeared at the gate that afternoon. We saw the family resemblance immediately: the same stocky build and smiley, open face.

"Is Calvin all right doing the night shift once a week?" I asked.

"He wasn't too keen, but reluctantly agreed."

I worried about this, but it was the only way we could see their shift system working. "I hope he'll be OK. I liked him: he's more mature…"

"Certainly than Henry!"

"…and looks strong, like he'll be able to put in a good day's physical work."

"Yeah, I think he'll be able to train Henry too, which is important."

Our final new employee was Tembo, hired to guard the plot at night. Each of the men worked a twelve-hour shift, although there was plenty of downtime. Only experience would tell us how competent they really were.

Our maids, Sherry and Precious, had already proven themselves and I didn't want to lose either of them with the move. Each in their own way was a candidate for the servants' quarters on the plot. The accommodation was large compared with some we had viewed. It had three rooms plus a kitchen and a separate toilet and shower, was in good condition and fairly recently whitewashed. The difficulty was in deciding which of them should live there. Sherry worked full time for us, was the elder and more experienced maid and currently lived furthest away in the house she was building for herself.

But the accommodation I had to offer was large for a single woman, and Precious had a husband and son and no home of her own. The extra rooms would be of more use to them and we'd also be helping the family financially.

I admired Sherry very much for her forward planning with the building of her own house. She'd begun before we arrived in Zambia and early on had told me that she needed us to stay for four years so she could complete the building. I was doing my best to make that a reality. The move lengthened her daily commute considerably and I was not willing to risk her looking for a job elsewhere.

In the end we put to them the idea of sharing the house. They'd always got on well, but I had my heart in my mouth when I made the suggestion. I needn't have worried: they smiled and, after a short chat, accepted the offer.

Every day I felt more and more settled in Zambia. It was almost two years since we'd first arrived in Lusaka: two years since we'd lost those passports; two years in a country I didn't want to be in; two years that I'd thought I'd count down every day; and two years since we'd moved into an empty house. Despite arriving with nothing, I'd had to employ a removal van in order to move all our belongings to the new house, a family home that would suit us for years. Zambia, the place I never wanted to come to, had grabbed hold of my ankles and wouldn't let me go. Instead of fleeing, I had plans to settle and stay. Stephen's six-month extension to his research was a start, and we were hopeful of a subsequent research grant. I had a good job, and the children were both settled at pre-school. The future looked more sorted than I ever imagined when I started out.

❧

Our new home had so much space we could afford to set aside a room as a study. It had a connecting door to the main bedroom, so I suspected it was originally designed as a nursing room for a new-born. For us it became the techno-hub of the house, which is a grand way of saying that it had a phone extension so we could connect the laptop to the internet.

One evening an unexpected email arrived. I ran to the living room to tell Stephen.

"Guess what! We've had an email from The Irish One."

For a time, before we were dating, Stephen and I had shared a flat with two others: The Irish One and Music Maestro. Both had their quirks, but The Irish One was in a league of his own. True to his heritage, he liked potatoes, though his cooking skills were limited. He would boil whole potatoes, by the kilogram, for hours in the biggest cooking pot the flat possessed. He was also responsible for melting the TV aerial while grilling bread, and took some pride in his madcap student exploit of carrying a bath up Arthur's Seat in order to slide down it. Graduating hadn't stopped his devil-may-care adventures, with a series of sporty cars being written off in the first year of employment. The style of car was probably more important than its credibility or safety.

"The Irish One? Seriously?" Stephen said. "What's he up to these days?"

"Well, I don't really know. He didn't say. But he's planning a world tour and would like to come and visit."

"Fabulous!" Stephen grinned from ear to ear. "When's he likely to arrive?"

"Late September, he thinks. It's all a little vague until he shores up the rest of the trip, but I think it will be after you get back from your conferences in Europe. And he's travelling with his sister. Did you ever meet her?"

"No, I don't think so."

We held a reverent pause while we considered how likely it was that she was as dangerous as her brother had been. Surely she would be a calming influence, reigning back the excesses? I decided it was almost impossible for anyone to be like him and said, "I'll say that's fine then?"

"Of course! Haven't seen him for ages! It would be good to find out what he's doing now."

With that, I dashed back to the study to confirm his visit.

❧

"Where I come from, Madam, we eat tortoises."

Calvin imparted this nugget of information while leaning on the rake, eyeing Thomas and TomFum with interest. I was sweating in the afternoon sun, trying to create appropriate shade and habitation for the tortoises in their newly built enclosure. They didn't have much of a home, just a bit of scrubland at the back of the swimming pool, and the leafy shrub I was planting had a negligible chance of survival given the rainy season had passed. It was not the first time Calvin had made this comment and I worried that one day I would come out to find the tortoises were missing.

"They are not there," I imagined Calvin would say, in a manner that stated the obvious while pretending to be helpful. "They have escaped," he would say, passing all the blame to Thomas and TomFum, the innocent victims. I would nod, and tell him to search the garden for them. This would, of course, have been a futile exercise, since the ground behind the house had grass a metre high. Finding two small tortoises would be nigh on impossible. Still, he would reluctantly look, feigning interest in locating them. Meanwhile, I would be left staring at the empty pen and remembering that their former owner had called one of them Houdini for a reason...

I shook my head. Calvin remained a mystery. His ability to vanish the moment some work in the garden was suggested was second to none. Well, maybe second to Henry, our other garden boy.

I replenished the tortoises' water supply and left them the ends of our vegetables and peelings. Straightening up, I suggested to Calvin that he got the long hose and gave my plant a good soaking before doing the same to the flower beds at the front. It was mid-May and we'd had the last rains of the year until October. The glistening greenery of the rainy season was fading and before long all the grass would be an arid brown. I wasn't very hopeful that my new plants would survive, not least because I depended upon Calvin and Henry to water them.

As I went inside for a long, cold drink, I wondered if *"What animals do you eat?"* ought to be on our list of interview questions, were the need ever to arise again.

It had tickled into June and the weather was getting cooler. In the city the coldest nights would fall to about 10°C mid-winter but the chill really got through to the bones.

I was not the only one to arrive at housegroup with chattering teeth and a warm jumper. Jenny obligingly shooed their furball out of the room and told Stephen which chair to avoid so his cat allergy wouldn't flare up.

"It's so cold!" I exclaimed. Somehow winter here got through to your bones. As I sat down, I took a mug of tea and cradled it, grateful for its warmth.

Eckhard smiled from across the room. "It is

astonishing, isn't it, how cold it is when the ambient room temperature falls below 28°C." His face was straight, but he had a twinkle in his eye.

My riposte was halted by the arrival of another friend, Todd, slightly out of breath from rushing.

"Gosh, you look frazzled!" Eckhard said.

Todd explained in his soft American accent how it had been non-stop at work that week and, in addition, the cat had had kittens.

"Again!" we exclaimed, almost in unison. It seemed like only last week that she'd produced her second litter, which he had assured us was going to be her last.

"Yes. Five of them." He paused and glanced round. "Anyone want a kitten?"

I joined the chorus of voices declining the offer, all of us very politely saying, "Thanks, but no thanks," apart from Stephen, who said, "We might be interested."

I stared at him in astonishment.

"In what way? You're allergic to cats!"

"Rats!" he said, not like a swear word but as a statement of fact. "We need a cat to ensure the plot is free of rats."

"Do we have many?" I asked fearfully.

"Oh! They are everywhere!" said Eckhard with a dismissive wave of his hand.

"Now I've dug that big hole for compost there's bound to be rats around," agreed Stephen.

"Eurgh!" I shivered. I'd been keen on the pit while I was saving the planet by getting rid of garden and kitchen waste. All of a sudden it didn't seem such a good idea.

Todd had been following this conversation with barely concealed amusement and knew which side his bread was buttered. Stephen asked him if his cat was a good ratter.

"She brings me plenty of gifts," he said, and the deal was done. Stephen said we'd take two (of indeterminate gender) and, this time, Todd swore their mother would have The Op. I began to panic. How on earth was I going to keep the cats from coming into the house? From lying on the bed? From curling up on the sofa? From… *from Calvin?*

No, Calvin's diet was surely limited to tortoises. *Wasn't it?*

Calvin's task for the day had been to water the garden and tend the plants we were trying to cultivate. He wandered past me and the tortoise enclosure, ambling down to the vegetable patch. That was his real forte, the place he most liked to be. Cynically I suspected it was because when there he could not be seen from the house. Life could move even slower when there was no *bwana* monitoring if you actually worked during your working hours.

To be fair, Calvin showed remarkable competency at watering. When water stopped flowing from the hosepipe he would go to investigate why. Henry, on the other hand, just stood there, holding the hose, waiting for the water to return. We had variable water pressure, so at certain times of the day and on certain parts of the plot it could be difficult to get any flow. Henry was given other duties, such as *sweep up all the leaves*, though his regular task of *switch the swimming pool pump off in the evening before you leave* was often left for Tembo to deal with when he arrived on night duty. It was a daily juggling act to get the jobs done: perhaps I shouldn't have expected miracles.

I liked to wander around the plot during the day. Not only did it keep Henry and Calvin on their toes, but I could see the areas that still needed work. Cutting down the grass at the back was a high priority, particularly as Sara had told me there were snakes in it. The children ran around freely and, although they were under strict instructions not to go out the back, since when have such rules been obeyed by adventurous pre-schoolers? Solving that anxiety merely resulted in the creation of a new one: machetes were needed to chop the grass. I feared the men would lose fingers and toes in the process, and knew that they were likely to leave the machetes lying around, particularly during one of their breaks. The children's carefree play could easily have found one of these lethal tools, and so inappropriate storage of machetes quickly became a sackable offence.

Mysteriously there was already a graveyard of gardening implements, even though nearly all of them had been bought new when we moved in only two months earlier. The metal rake had a funny slant to it and two water sprinklers were damaged beyond reasonable repair. The 'push-and-click' hosepipe connections remained an impossibility for the gardeners, despite three detailed tutorials. They were both also astonished that the secateurs were unable to prune the thick branches of the long-established avocado tree, the assault causing near fatal damage to both plant and implement.

There was a beep at the gate and Calvin ran up the drive to let the car in. It was Stephen, home from work for the day. Delighted by his unexpectedly early return and given the sun was rapidly approaching the yardarm, I poured us both a gin and tonic and asked him to stroll around the plot with me. We were still learning our responsibilities. Freed from the shade of the mulberry tree I relished the large open garden our new plot offered. I had to admit that the garden didn't look too bad and the vegetable patch had life in it.

"Any idea what these are?" Stephen asked, pointing at some scrubby plants just outside our bedroom window.

"Not a clue. Calvin watered the bed this morning, but it looks a little bare. Perhaps we could visit that garden centre near the shop that sells cheese, back in Kabulonga, and get something to fill in the gaps?"

"Sounds a good plan. What do you think would work?"

I practically snorted my drink out through my nose. "You're asking me advice about plants?"

We were both novice gardeners in the UK: in Zambia we were a level below that.

"I live in hope," Stephen said, moving on to look at some of the well-established trees. He was only interested in ones that bore fruit. We recognised the paw paw (or papaya), as we'd had a couple of smaller versions at our old house. There were two avocados: one in the front garden and one shadowing the vegetable plot. The driveway had yet more paw paw, a guava and a lemon tree.

The grass jungle at the back of the house had three trees curving along the path to where our maids lived. Here I was able to tell Stephen what a friend from church had told me earlier.

"She thinks these are apple trees."

"Apple trees? Here? In Zambia?"

"Yep!"

"I didn't think they were a tropical plant?"

"No, she said they weren't. Apparently they need a frost in order to rest and then fruit in season, which is why they don't grow easily in this part of the world."

Stephen inspected the leaves. "Looks healthy enough," he muttered, before turning his attention to the biggest tree on the plot, which must have been standing behind the tennis court for many years. It had an ovoid shaped fruit and some dying branches. On closer inspection we realised that was due to termites, the lower half of the trunk coloured terracotta with their dusty deposits.

"What did she say this was?"

"Didn't know. Can you reach any of the fruit?"

At full stretch, Stephen could just about pull down one of the lower branches. With some effort and a sharp tug the fruit came off, a firm rugby ball of unappetising solidity. He turned it over in his hands, sniffing it and staring at the yellowy-green skin. "It doesn't smell of anything," he said. "I suggest we cut it up in the kitchen and see what's inside."

Turning round, he noticed a couple of thorny bushes, sprouting madly, like Einstein's hair. "And what are these?" he asked

I shrugged. "I don't remember seeing them before. Calvin must have cleared that section of grass." I inspected them closely. Nothing but weak, spiky branches. "Another wait-and-see, though they're mighty ugly."

The grass-clearing machete was in use again shortly, as the kitchen knife was inadequate for cutting through the mystery fruit. When we eventually opened it up, it revealed five pockets with white (evidently unripe) nut-like pods.

"Well," I said, poking at the spongy padding, "I'm none the wiser."

"Time for the internet," declared Stephen, heading down the corridor to the study to connect while I hurriedly made dinner. Precious had bathed the children and they were running riot around the living room in the pyjamas.

"Shush, you two!" I said in mock horror at their behaviour. "Fancy some *Balamory*?"

"Yes please!" Matthew screamed, and immediately rushed to sit on the sofa. Eleanor giggled and followed her brother, climbing up beside him while I fiddled with the video player. Television on, I turned round to see my babies snuggled up together, Eleanor sucking her thumb, her elder brother with his arm protectively round her, both contentedly staring at the TV.

THE SPICE BOYS

As ever, on our return from holiday Sherry was there to greet us as we staggered in through the back door. We'd had two weeks in the Spice Island of Zanzibar, made all the more exciting as we travelled there by train. Sherry swiftly took our suitcases to the bedrooms and, as anticipated, was more interested in greeting the children than us. Very soon they were running around together, catching up on their fortnight apart.

While they were getting reacquainted, I put the kettle on for a mug of tea. Evidently Sherry had only just refilled the top section of the water filter as I struggled to eke out enough of the clean, filtered water to stretch to two mugs. I thought it would be nice to sit out on the terrace at the front to drink our tea so, while the kettle boiled, I went to unlock the padlock for the door out of the living room.

I should explain the layout of the house. At the back was a carport, from which there was a door into the utility room and then the kitchen. This was our usual entrance and exit: the tradesman's entrance, if you like. When approaching the house from the front, you walked past the living room, which had two external doors in a wall of glass windows, to reach the front door. This opened onto a small entrance hall (which in turn had doors to the kitchen straight ahead, the living room off to the right and to the left was the corridor that led to the bedrooms) but we had never used this entrance. It seemed daft, when we had to walk past the two living room doors to reach it.

The first of these doors had always been locked. In true Zambian style, a teaspoon held the hinge together and we never felt confident enough to risk it as our daily thoroughfare. It also opened awkwardly onto the path. Instead we used the second door. Unlike the first, there wasn't a key for the lock but, like every other door and window in the house, there was a security grille inside, so our safety was based upon padlocking the metal grilles.

Three possible front doors, and our chosen method of entry and exit was the door without a lock. Sometimes it was hard to explain the logic in our thinking.

Having removed the padlock and opened the grille, I depressed the handle and pushed the door.

It didn't move. I tried again – jiggling it, shaking it a little – but nothing happened. I was baffled.

"Sherry!"

"Yes, Madam?" She came running.

"Do you know what's happened here?"

"Precious locked it," she said.

Incredulous, I questioned, "Locked it?"

"Yes, Madam."

141

"But how?" I wasn't angry (after all, locking a main door is a perfectly reasonable thing to do) but there was no key. When we'd moved in we'd tried all we'd been given, and (because I was aware that in Zambia keys did seem to work in a variety of locks) all the others we could find. Perhaps she had found an alternative?

But Sherry didn't know which key and, when called upon, neither did Precious. She said she used one of the keys on the ring, so we tried all of them again to no avail.

It was a mystery never to be solved. The padlock was put back in place and we resorted to using the official front door. That had a very normal, five-lever mortice lock and we began to wonder why we had never used it before.

~

Returning from holiday brought additions to the family. Firstly, leaving the fish to their own devices had been foolish. Six had become eight, though it crossed my mind that other small friends may have also appeared but been eaten. Probably not something to discuss in front of the children.

Then Todd's kittens finally arrived. After their due period of weaning, he gave us two black cats, one with a little white splodge of fur. Their basket was put in the garage, just outside the back door. Everyone was on high alert to shoo them out of the house so Stephen's allergy to cats wouldn't flare. Warning Sherry and Precious of the importance of keeping the cats out of the house turned out to be premature, as for days neither of the kittens moved from their new home. The children loved them and spent ages sitting on the concrete floor beside the basket, stroking their furry backs. There was no evidence that Stephen's allergy had been passed on. I liked to think that was due to my superior genes but Stephen insisted it was pure luck.

Two cats, two tortoises and eight fish. You would be forgiven for thinking this would be enough. But I succumbed to an advert in the window at the bakery.

"Labrador pups for sale."

There was one left.

I had been pondering the idea of a puppy for a while. My children had both developed a mild fear of dogs. I'm sure it was mainly because they were about the same height and found it quite frightening to have one bounding up to them. A puppy, I thought, would definitely be smaller than them, and they could grow up with it and hopefully overcome their phobia.

I took the family on a trip to the farm where the litter had been born. It was quite a journey so I decided on the spot to take the last puppy home with us. It became imperative as the children instantly loved the cute puppy, though Stephen kept muttering the warning, "A puppy is for life, not just for Christmas."

"It'll be fine," I said, dismissing his anxieties. I'd grown up with dogs my father had trained magnificently. How difficult could a little puppy be?

୧

He was barking again. It was the middle of the night – the third consecutive night of broken sleep – and, being winter, it was cold. I did not want to have to pad down to the utility room again, a process that involved unlocking a number of security padlocks en route.

"Stephen! Stephen! Wake up!" I nudged my husband awake.

"Urgh?"

"The dog's barking. Can you go and settle him?"

"Urgh?" He shuffled around a bit. "OK," he

grunted, eyes still closed. Seconds later he was sound asleep.

My dog: my responsibility.

In the morning I was not particularly receptive to Stephen's banter as he brought me tea in bed.

"Come on, love, wake up. Here's a cup of tea. Isn't it marvellous that the dog slept through the night, only barking a little before six?"

If I could have kept my eyes open long enough they would have shot daggers at him. Instead he blithely went his merry way back to the kitchen to prepare breakfast.

Laboriously, I dragged myself into a sitting position, drank my tea and considered the next move of getting out of bed. I heard the children chattering away so knew that I could not rest for long. They had to get to pre-school and I had to go to work. I plodded wearily through to the kitchen.

"We have to do something about the dog," I said.

Stephen looked quizzically at me.

"Barking," I added. "All night."

"Oh," he said, still blissfully unaware that there had been noise.

"He just wants company, I suppose," I said, running my hands through my unruly hair, "but I don't want to let him into the bedrooms."

When I was a child the rule my father had insisted on was that our dog never went upstairs, and certainly never went into the bedrooms. Here it was a little more difficult, as we were in a bungalow. However, the bedrooms were along one corridor and, as long as we remembered to shut the door, the dog could be kept to the living and kitchen area quite easily.

Stephen refilled my mug as a peace offering. He was clearly more awake than I, and therefore the one with the brilliant idea.

"Why don't we leave him with Tembo? He would be good company for Tembo – possibly even keep him awake!"

"Excellent! He can become a guard dog, though I'm not sure our daft puppy will scare anyone away."

"He'll jump up and knock them over with his enthusiastic greeting. Then lick them to death. Burglars stand no chance."

Stephen had, as so often, brought a smile to my face when I least expected it. When I wanted to grump and groan, his wit and humour banished the black cloud and calmly brought normality.

Two small bundles of energy rushed past me heading straight for the puppy.

"Morning kids!" called Stephen. They uttered some sort of reply, but their focus was elsewhere.

"Matthew, leave the poor animal alone." The puppy cowered in a corner, abandoning the food Stephen had left out. Mind you, it was the local version of Weetabix and my breakfast option too. After two years of nothing but this cardboard monstrosity, my toleration of it was low. Should the dog be judged for sharing my distaste?

Reluctantly Matthew returned to the kitchen and climbed up on the stool at the breakfast bar. I passed him his cereal and milk.

"Mummy can we call him Thomas?"

"No, darling, that's a silly name."

"It's not. It's what we've called the tortoises."

I hated being floored by four-year-old logic.

"Ye-es, which is a good reason for not giving the dog the same name. Besides, it also needs to be a good name for calling, so that he will be obedient and well trained. When I was growing up our dogs were named after sweets. I had Fudge, and my friend's dog was called Truffle, and then our second dog was Barley, like barley sugar." Conspiratorially I whispered to Matthew, "I always wanted her to be called Toffee, not Barley, but I was outvoted. Could we call our new puppy Toffee?"

Stephen chipped in. "I thought he should be named after a spice, given our recent holiday. Maybe the cats too." Turning to Matthew he asked, "Can you remember going round the spice farm?"

Matthew looked blankly at his father. Less than a fortnight on and it was a memory that was vanishing.

"I don't know – all this cultural input and it's all wasted on them," I declared in dismay.

Ignoring us both, Stephen said, "I'll see what Google offers us," and marched off to the office.

While he busied himself with spice name research, I downed my mug of tea and chivvied the children along. Naming the menagerie could wait until a little later in the day.

ॐ

My family's first puppy had arrived when I was a similar age to Matthew, maybe a couple of years older. We'd acquired the dog at a weekend and in Monday's school duty of writing my 'news' I'd mentioned the dog's arrival. The teacher picked up on this and asked the class for suggestions for names. Much to my parents' amusement, a group of five-year-olds had suggested Brandy, Rum and Whisky at the top of their list. Fudge had been way down.

The sweet heritage was lost though and the spice boy won. After collating a list of spices we settled for Mustard, thinking that our golden Labrador looked a little like a dirty French mustard colour. To keep the spicy theme going the cats were called Nutmeg and Mace, two spices from the one plant. Fortunately we didn't also have to name each individual fish.

Stephen's googled research, together with a hint from our spice farm tour, had finally defined the mystery fruit from our garden.

"You won't believe it, but I think it's a cocoa pod," he told me.

"You mean we can make chocolate?" I asked, open-eyed with excitement.

"Well," he cautioned, "I looked that up too. Seems they need roasting and go through quite complicated treatment before they are ready to turn into chocolate. Sorry."

"Darn! That could have saved us a fortune!" I said.

"Talking of saving money, what do you think about getting chickens?" Stephen asked. "There's a nice patch under the big tree at the end of the tennis court where..." Seeing my face, his voice petered out. Maybe we had enough for now.

STEALING THE SHOW

The school year was drawing to a close. One afternoon Matthew told me about the upcoming end of term show. I certainly wouldn't dare miss such a prestigious piece of local theatre. With great seriousness and pride he told me, "I'm an actorrator."

I couldn't bring myself to question or disillusion him, and was rescued by an almighty crash in the kitchen. I ran through to find one of the ceiling boards had fallen in, bringing with it a mound of dust, dirt and the root cause: termites. Termites were everywhere in Zambia. We knew we had them in the garden, creeping up the trunk of the cocoa tree. They were renowned for eating through almost anything: plants, wood, concrete – in fact, only metal seemed to deter these voracious consumers. In the bush their existence formed part of the ecology and assisted some plant and bird life. In the town they were cursed for their destructive habits. Looking at the critters sprayed over the floor and work surfaces, I assumed the neighbouring panels would also be laden with them, as probably was much of the roof void. It had been a threat ever since we moved in; the ceiling's gentle bowing deepening in recent days.

But I hadn't anticipated the rest of the week's dramas.

જ

There was a knock at the back door. Calvin stood, head bowed, fiddling with his cap.

"Madam, Tembo's not arrived."

"Really? Do we know why not?"

"No, Madam."

I could tell Calvin didn't want to tell me this news, and I certainly didn't want to hear it. If Tembo wasn't there then we had no night guard on duty. No night guard meant no security, and I'd heard enough tales of burglaries to want someone to patrol the plot.

I drew my breath. "Calvin, I'm really sorry, but you'll have to stay. I'll pay you, of course." I hated doing this to him. He'd already worked a twelve-hour shift of physical toil in the garden (well, fairly physical – for him) and now I was expecting him to stay another twelve hours overnight.

"OK, Madam." He trudged off to put his bits and pieces away before retreating to the shelter by the gate.

As I went back to preparing dinner I considered my situation. Calvin on duty that night was not much more security than an empty gate, given he was most likely to sleep. I thought of changing my mind and letting him go, but then realised that I was more likely to sleep if he was there than if he wasn't. Selfishly I took my sleep

149

above his.

My fears were unfounded. Tembo turned up at about the time we were going to bed, making some garbled excuse to Stephen.

"He was chasing someone who stole from his home while he wasn't there, and who took the mattress, and his wife is elsewhere and… well, I don't really understand, but it doesn't sound good."

I stared at him. It made no sense. "I'll ask Precious later," I said.

"Probably best," he said ruefully. "Meanwhile I've let Calvin go home and locked everything up for the night. Time to sleep."

Regardless of the evening's uncertainty with the guards, and the mystifying explanation from Tembo for his absence, I slept well with no lingering thoughts about our security. When Precious arrived late morning the story was a lot clearer.

"Someone came to Tembo's house last night," she told me as she began the laundry. "They were demanding money that Tembo says he hadn't borrowed."

Tembo had been here on the plot, at work. That left his wife alone in their house, facing this unwelcome man. She didn't open the door but screamed for help, which brought her neighbours running and scared the man off. Then she went to stay with one of them.

"Thank goodness for that!" I exclaimed.

"Yes, but the men returned while she was out. In the morning she found they had broken down the door and stolen everything: the mattress, two suitcases of clothes and two new cooking pots."

"Oh no!" I bit my lower lip, thinking hard. What struck me as awful was the cooking pots. They needed those to cook nshima and relish, the staple food. Without them, how would Mrs Tembo cook and feed her family?

"What can we do, Precious?"

She shrugged her shoulders and returned to the washing. "I don't know," she replied over her shoulder.

I asked Stephen the same question later.

"What can we do?"

"Nothing much," he said.

"I could give him a saucepan." I realised that this was scant help but I had some old pans that I rarely used. Surely something for Mrs Tembo was better than nothing? "At least they've still got their home," I muttered, almost to myself.

Stephen put down his book with a sigh.

"Yes, but not much of one, with a door broken down and nothing left in it."

"It must be horrible to be on your own, night after night," I was still thinking of Mrs Tembo and her children. While Tembo turned up dutifully for work every evening, they were left alone to fend for themselves. My conscience smarted at my own actions, because when Tembo hadn't turned up I'd made Calvin stay, so that I would feel safe.

Could it be right to leave a family like that?

Then again, if I didn't employ Tembo he would not have the money to pay for food, let alone new cooking pots. He would have had no money for a home and the whole family would have been in further poverty and debt. Night guard involved no education and no real skills (though we asked Tembo to water the lawn, if only to keep him awake). His night-time work also might have freed his wife to take a daytime job.

I took the weight of their problems upon my shoulders, unaware that I'd be facing yet another moral conundrum after coffee the following day.

Kelly and I met at the café to put the world to rights while her children happily played with Lego beside us.

It was a shame mine were missing a playdate by being at pre-school, but I was glad of the chance to chat. She allayed my worries about Tembo and his family with her wisdom about Africa. Kelly had been here many more years than me and had a much more pragmatic approach. The morning's downtime had cost a bit (a combined consumption of tea, coffee, hot chocolate, milkshakes and plenty of cake) but it was worth it.

The waitress brought me the bill. In total, it was accurate, but I was surprised that, rather than having it all typed out on the till receipt, a couple of items were added in pen at the bottom. Nevertheless, I couldn't quibble over the amount (more's the pity!) and dutifully paid it.

But I kept the receipt.

After Kelly and her children had left I went to the counter and spoke with the owner, who I knew quite well through my regular visits to her café and her family's bakery.

"I'm a bit concerned about the bill," I said.

She looked at the bill in horror. "No," she said. "Can I keep it?"

"Of course. I've paid the full amount, so you know."

"Thank you. And thank you for showing me this."

"No problem!"

I left and took a whirlwind trip round the supermarket before going home. As I walked down the shopping mall back to the car I was accosted by a black woman who stepped in front of me, stopping me in my path.

"You've lost me my job. What are you going to do about it?" she spat out.

It took me a moment to recognise her as the waitress who had served me in the café. I stared at her, lost for words.

"I'm very sorry to hear that," I stuttered.

"Yeah, right," she sneered.

"I am," I insisted. I didn't like to see anyone out of a job and that hadn't been my intention, even if logic dictated the probability. "But what you did was wrong," I said, as gently as possible.

"Look at me!" she said, pointing at her stomach. My heart sank still further. With my usual lack of observation I hadn't registered that she was pregnant. "Look at me! Waitressing does not pay well and I have a family to support, so I just needed a little extra. Why did you have to say anything? No-one was harmed."

I bit my lip, biding my time. Wherever you live, waitressing is never a highly paid job. I'm sure she was earning a pittance. But did that give her the right to appropriate more? I tried to absorb her anger and speak as calmly as possible. I repeated softly that what she did was wrong and tried to explain the simple economics. Her wage might not have been enough for her to live comfortably, but that was no reason to take money from customers that should go to the owner.

Her anger at losing her job was far too raw for my logic to have any impact.

"So what are you going to do?" she demanded again. "Can you go and speak with her, give me back my job?"

"No, that is for her and you to sort out. Now if you'll excuse me, I'm going home."

Rather than force my way past her, I turned to leave, taking a circuitous route to the car. I heard her hurling abuse at me with every step I took.

On arriving home I realised I was shaking. It might have been less than an hour since I'd last sat down for a drink, but I made myself a cup of tea and took it outside. Sitting on the terrace gazing at the garden always calmed me down. There I could think and nature could heal me. I had no guilty conscience about what I had done, but I did feel for the waitress and her unborn child. She was struggling to make a decent wage for her family and I had put an end to that, even if she had caused the downfall herself. It hammered home to me once again that I was 'wealthy white' not 'poor black' and still this mattered: I was in the position of power and she was in the position of weakness.

Then I wept for her, for Tembo, and for the harsh economies of the land.

ॐ

Although one of the reasons for moving house had been to create a bit of space between us and Gwyn, her move to live in the school opposite meant we frequently caught up. She often came over late afternoon and played with the children. Usually Gareth came too, now a permanent fixture in all our lives. Matthew and Eleanor adored him: Gareth gladly filled the uncle role of 'doing things your parents would never allow but you ought to do anyway'.

On this particular day he had taken them for a swim while I made dinner. Gwyn was pouring us all some drinks when Stephen came home from work, unexpectedly early. He looked dreadful, greeting us cursorily as he walked past with his bags.

"What's up with him?" Gwyn asked.

"I haven't a clue," I said. It was most out of character, particularly if his sister was around.

Gwyn picked up the Mosi and said, "I'll take this to Gareth and leave him to you."

"Thanks," I said wryly to her disappearing body.

"You're welcome," she called over her shoulder with a grin.

I judiciously took another Mosi from the fridge and went to find my husband. He was sitting on the sofa, staring absently at the fireplace.

"Here, this is for you," I said, proffering the beer.

He took it without a word. Something had to be seriously wrong.

"What's up?" I asked, sitting down beside him.

Stephen held his head in his hands, staring with a glazed look at the floor. "Honestly, it seems to be one thing after another. First the DVDs and now–" He shook his head.

The DVD reference was to a parcel that we had ordered from the UK. The courier system usually worked well, but when Stephen went to pick up this particular parcel at the weekend the box looked suspiciously tampered with. There was additional sellotape around it, not like our usual deliveries. Sure enough, on opening it we found one of the DVDs we'd ordered was missing. We could only assume that either Customs & Excise had taken it when calculating the duty or it was somebody at the courier company. Obviously Stephen queried the issue at the desk, but they pointed to their terms and conditions, claiming no responsibility for loss or damage. It seemed a fine line between loss and theft; we had no choice but to take the cost on the chin.

Slowly Stephen's story came out, and explained why he was home early. Losing a DVD box set had been bad but the cause of his current misery was far worse. His laptop had been stolen from his laboratory office.

"Why didn't I lock it to the desk as usual?" he shouted in frustration.

What could I say? Neither of us could turn back time. I put my arms around him. All I could offer was a moment of stillness and calm.

Eventually he raised his head. "Thanks," he said and gave me a hug.

Reaching for his drink I could see the despair wash over him once again.

"Tell me what happened," I asked gently.

He took a sip of his beer, then a deep breath, and told the tale.

"I'd been working in the lab early on, then had to go to the ward to see some patients and for a meeting with Mwiya." Mwiya had a fantastic Zambian name. He really was Dr Mwiya Mwiya. I could tell Stephen was down because we didn't have our customary enjoyment of repeating his name, wrapping our tongues around the syllable repetition.

"I was late," he continued, "and so I didn't bother to lock my laptop."

The laboratory was the opposite end of the hospital from the children's wards – easily a twenty-minute walk, and actually the main reason we bought The Professor, so Stephen wouldn't waste time running back and forwards. Most of his work was in the lab, as he analysed all the data from his patients. It was Dr Mwiya's responsibility to be the on-site doctor for the children, but they had regular meetings and Stephen was often on the ward helping out with diagnoses, regimes and protocols.

Stephen employed an assistant in the lab, who typed one-fingered at the pace of a snail. Nevertheless, he was diligent with his work. Others worked there as well, working on different projects, and despite the small size of the office a lot of people passed through. Medicine, and in particular research, is a very collaborative subject. Partly because of the uncertainty as to who would be in the office, Stephen had invested in a special metal chain and lock that prevented his laptop from being physically removed. That extra security had felt essential from early in our stay in Zambia, and that was part of why he was cursing himself. The one time he didn't lock it securely was the occasion it was stolen.

"When I got back, it was gone. No-one claims to

know anything." Stephen looked to the skies, but we both knew that couldn't be true. Someone must have seen something. It was remarkably opportunistic that a third party was able to sneak in and take a laptop without anyone noticing anything suspicious.

Stephen smiled a wry smile. "I called the police, of course, and it is being overseen by the local CID. He claims he was trained at Scotland Yard. I've spent all afternoon driving him around and, where he needed to be on his own, I've paid for the taxis and phonecards."

"Do you expect a result? A conviction, or – better still – retrieval of the computer?"

"What do you think?" he spat out, with a hollow laugh. "No. I think it's a façade. It's probably an inside job, and on one level I'm not sure I want to know who. How's that going to help when I'm working there?"

It wouldn't. He'd lost some confidence in his colleagues. Would a conviction make it any better? They'd probably gang up on him to make his life more miserable. There was one law of God and the land: do not steal. There was another of your people: stick together against the outsider.

Stephen sighed. "Well, they're not going to get far with it. They don't have the power cable and can't possibly know the passwords so it's almost useless to anyone else. And it's a Mac, so will stand out a mile here in Zambia."

"Have you phoned your supervisor?"

His face fell again. "No, that's the job for this evening. I'm dreading it." Stephen went quiet. The last thing he wanted was to look foolish in front of his supervisor in the UK. Stephen had so much respect and admiration for him, so this was one disaster he didn't want to admit to.

"It'll be fine," I said, squeezing his hand. I could hear squeals of laughter from the swimming pool and knew our time together would be interrupted soon. A thought struck me. "Gareth may know someone who can help – he works in IT. Why not ask him? Go and join them all for a swim while I finish dinner. See if he and Gwyn can stay to eat."

"But I need to phone the UK."

"You can do that later. A couple of hours won't make any difference now."

I stood up and held my hand out for his empty bottle. He was still fiddling with it, drumming his fingers against the glass, picking at the label.

"Come on," I persuaded him. "The children will take your mind off things. Even if for a short while, that's a good thing."

He passed me the bottle and stood up. "You're right. I'll go and see what they're up to."

I heard a loud splash and then a wail.

"I think you might be needed quickly!"

"On my way," he called, already halfway out the door.

❧

The pre-school end of year production was underway. I was squashed into the airless music room between other mothers whose pride was fighting for space with mine. Despite the jostling and the heat, I felt more comfortable here than I had outside earlier in the week. That had been Sports Day. Matthew had done well, actually winning one race of the four he was competing in. He hadn't done so well at the egg and spoon though: he'd held onto the spoon rather than the egg. Oh, the penalties for following the rules.

Eleanor, my bubbly blonde two-and-a-half-year-old, had been a lot less focused. She was only in one race and had to be persuaded to run at all. She came second (of two) largely because she had been busy grinning and waving at her mum rather than concentrating on getting to the finish line.

This escapade had drawn attention to my presence, so I'd been unable to avoid the Mums' Race. There is nothing so competitive in mothering as the race on Sports Day. I'd been utterly unprepared; a dozen others were in tracksuits and trainers. I'd felt obliged to show some willingness to compete and so took off my sandals in order to run, but my long flowing skirt was never going to be the most practical outfit. Beside me had been Laura, another mother who I knew slightly. She had been equally underdressed, underprepared and underwhelmed by the experience.

"Don't worry," I said, "you won't be last."

"Oh, yes I think I will," she said. "I know! How about we have a pact and cross the line together?"

"Great idea!"

And the race had begun.

Laura and I were equally good, swiftly falling to the back of the race.

And then I'd suddenly thought: *I could run a little faster than this.* And so I did.

Until I heard a voice beside me calling, "Wait for me!"

And so, a shade reluctantly, I did – and, holding hands aloft, we'd crossed the finish line together.

In last place.

Of course my best support had come from my son, never one to mince words.

"Mum, you were terrible."

I was on more solid ground in the school music room. A row of face-painted children took a bow as I joined everyone else in a thunderous round of applause. Finally I was introduced to actorrating. Matthew had stood at the side and narrated, filling in the gaps between the destruction of houses and then the wolf in *The Three Little Pigs*. He delivered his lines confidently and waited impatiently for the pigs to do their part. Inexplicably, actorrating also required bright blue blobs of paint on his face. Afterwards, I discovered that the teachers had used ordinary poster paint, which was almost impossible to remove. Eleanor (as a currant bun, one of five in the baker's shop) had stained red spots on her face for days.

As the applause died down the headmaster came forward to praise our golden children. He had come into his profession via the education of 17-18 year-olds and was amusingly uncomfortable surrounded by pre-schoolers. Then Matthew's class were shuffled out, and returned one-by-one to be presented with a certificate. This was a proper graduation, as they now wore black gowns and had mortarboards on their heads.

When Matthew's name was called, I grinned from ear to ear, welling up with pride for my boy. Yes, all the children performed well; and yes, I was not the only mother with a child graduating to 'big school'; and yes, the mortarboard thing was utterly ridiculous. Nevertheless, for me the actorrator had stolen the show.

A LETTER HOME

Dear Matthew and Eleanor,

There aren't any postcards here to buy, or send, so I thought I'd write you a letter. I'm currently staying in a hotel in Lubumbashi. I've stayed here before – in a different room, but they are all very similar. It has a bed, and a chest of drawers and a wardrobe.

The funniest thing, though, is the toilet. It is almost part of the room, just separated by a shower curtain! It would never pass Health & Safety in the UK! As I'm on my own I don't mind too much, but it would be uncomfortable if I was sharing. What if Daddy did a big poo – eurgh!

I smiled, as I could picture my son squirming at that thought and then laughing raucously.

The room also has a television, but not many channels to

watch.

I refrained from telling my children that all I was able to tune in to on this visit were porn channels, or scantily dressed ladies encouraging me to phone the number on the screen. I'd had a quick flick through in the hope of something of quality, then switched it off. On previous visits I'd used spare time such as this to read a novel – precious peace without children to interrupt - but that evening I felt inspired to write them a letter instead. Of course they couldn't read yet, so it was written as much to amuse and entertain Stephen.

The other reason I can't watch the TV is that here in the DRC they speak French. I did a bit of French at school and understand a little, but never quite enough. I have learnt, though, that they have a special word for 90 here. In the French I learnt, the numbers gradually increased in length as well as size so, for example, 60 was soixante but 70 was soixante-dix (or 60 + 10). Similarly 80 was quatre-vingts (four twenties) and 90 was quatre-vingt-dix (80 + 10). By the time I reached 99 I was exhausted: quatre-vingt-dix-neuf. The sensible people of the DRC have chosen to abbreviate 70 and 90 to septante and nonante respectively – much easier (when I remember!).

This is all too difficult for you just now, but I'll remember to tell you when you are old enough to understand. Perhaps you'll prefer to live in the DRC than in France?

Somehow I doubted that: I suspected age and common sense would intervene. But I'd be happy to visit them in Mauritius…

I am making good use of my French-English dictionary that I got when I was sitting exams many years ago. Then I had simple phrases of greeting (Bonjour) and to say what I was doing or liked (Je suis à l'école. J'aime jouer du violoncelle.) Now I am having to learn business phrases so I can converse with a lawyer and, possibly, a bank manager.

I was in the Democratic Republic of the Congo (DRC) on business, finalising the set up of a company for my boss and his colleague. Though employed by only one of them in Zambia, here I was employed by them both, which sometimes made it a little difficult to balance my loyalties. They were great people and needed each other for the new company to work. What I needed was more understanding of business French!

Did you know that here in Lubumbashi there is a roundabout with an elephant in the middle? A statue, not a real one, of course. Imagine what it would be like if a real elephant was in the middle of a busy roundabout!

The traffic was pretty crazy around the elephant. I'm not even sure anyone knew which way round the roundabout they were supposed to go. I was most grateful that I never had to drive.

My favourite place, though, is a crêperie. Crêpes with nutella and banana are my special treat when we're here. There's also a nice place to go for pizza. The more I think about it, the more I think you'd like it here!

Pizza and chocolate: what could go wrong, at least as far as a four-year-old boy was concerned?

Of course, much did go wrong in the DRC. I sat back from my letter-writing and thought about this troubled country. It was embattled with tribal fighting in the east of the country, merging with the Hutu/Tutsi divisions on the Rwanda and Burundi borders. At that time it had the largest UN Peacekeeping Force in the world, and still there were skirmishes and appalling, torturous deaths.

Since it was first suggested I might have to visit the DRC, I had read up on some of its history. It had never managed to establish itself after independence from Belgian colonial rule. King Leopold had owned the country, having sought land in the carving up of Africa by European powers. Africa was so rich in resources that the Western powers fought to control as much as they could. Leopold was no saint, and the indigenous people were keen to be rid of him. Following serious riots in the capital, Leopardsville (now Kinshasa), independence was granted in June 1960 with Patrice Lumumba as Prime Minister.

He didn't hold the post for long. A month later the army mutinied and Katanga – the province I was staying in – declared independence. Belgium sent in their army, ostensibly to protect Belgian citizens and mining interests. By September the President Kasavubu had dismissed Lumumba as Prime Minister and in December he was arrested. The following February he was brutally murdered, allegedly with the US and Belgium complicit in the assassination. It was a brief period at the top for the man who had brought about his country's independence.

During the fight for independence, he had been friends with a certain Joseph Mobutu. Four years after Lumumba's murder, Mobutu seized power through a coup, then held dictatorial control for over thirty years, principally through blatantly corrupt practices. Initially his charisma carried him, rousing the citizens with his broadcast speeches. He prided himself in his African heritage, no longer wearing western clothes (the jacket-and-tie was all but outlawed) and renamed himself Mobutu Sese Seko, removing his Christian name. He also renamed the country and the river that curves through it Zaire. Mobutu's legacy was a united nation;

but 'Zairean sickness' came to mean gross corruption, theft and mismanagement. The country's infrastructure was destroyed.

When Laurent-Désiré Kabila led a force from the Eastern Province in 1997, following the course of the Congo river, Mobutu's days were done. Kabila took over the capital and reverted the country's name to the Democratic Republic of the Congo. But the DRC just could not find peace. Within months, rebels backed by Rwanda and Uganda advanced on Kinshasa. Angola, Zimbabwe and Namibia backed Kabila. It was a further year before a multinational ceasefire accord was signed in Lusaka, Zambia. I smiled with pride at the peacemaking record of my adopted home.

But the ceasefire didn't end the country's violent unhappiness. Laurent Kabila was shot by his own bodyguard in 2001 and succeeded by his son, Joseph. One of the things that struck me, while staying in this troubled land, was that it was ruled by a man who was younger than me. It was not a job I would have dreamt of applying for: he inherited a terrifying mess of tribalism, corruption and violence.

I returned to my letter, and the reason I was here: the riches below ground.

Lubumbashi used to be called Elisabethville, but was renamed by former President Mobutu. It is just the other side of the border, in the strip of the DRC that mirrors the Zambian Copperbelt region. Its wealth comes from copper extracted from the land. There is a huge mine on the edge of the city, which I could see as we came in to land. It is so big that the waste from digging the mine has created a mountain of its own. This slag heap has a road up the side and a building towards the top. When I first saw it, I couldn't understand why anyone would want to live on a black mountain!

I was subsequently told that over the years they had developed better ways of extracting copper from the rocks they mine, so much so that it was now cost-efficient to re-process the slag heap. The house I saw was actually a guard's hut and offices, and the road carried trucks and lorries up and down laden with copper ore.

I have spent most of this trip in our offices in Kolwezi. The DRC is so big you need to fly between the major cities. Kinshasa, the capital, is 1500 kilometres to the north-west of here but it is thick forest terrain the whole way. It would take weeks, even in a car, to get there – and that assumes you could buy fuel en route. And Kinshasa is only about halfway up the country. So in the DRC you either fly, or go by boat along the Congo river... which doesn't come near here... We flew.

The offices in Kolwezi were a sight to behold. I had been told they needed 'a woman's touch' and that was an understatement. The main room had the murkiest brown carpet, a relic from the 1970s, and roughcast plastering on the walls sharp enough to cut yourself on when passing. In the middle of the room was (inexplicably) a pillar, beside which was a brass bucket and pipework leading up to the ceiling, and eventually out of one of the walls. It all looked a little bizarre but was a practical heat conduction system, the idea being that a fire would be lit in the bucket and the heat transferred around the room and house. In thirty-five-degree heat this seemed an unnecessary extravagance but the locals told me that the temperature dropped in the winter months.

For me, there was a hint of home with the plumbing system, which creaked, groaned and had unreliable water pressure. When there was little running water, the toilets had to be 'flushed' from a bucket. At that point I hadn't realised how much I would need to get used to this system of waste disposal.

I'd been taken to an exploration site while I was there. Again, I was grateful not to be driving, as the roads disintegrated as soon as we left the town. The Landcruiser was normally used for transporting miners and geologists, together with all their dirt and equipment. I was in the back of the vehicle in my sunniest summer dress. There was a padded bench seat running the length of the vehicle, where I sat and hung on to a strap dangling from the ceiling. After a while my arm began to ache so I let go, until we went over a ferocious pothole and I was flung to the floor. The men in the front didn't even notice: so much for gentlemanly chivalry!

The back seat was more attractive when we reached a police checkpoint. Zambia had these too, but they didn't feel as intimidating as the ones in the DRC. Perhaps I was used to the Zambian way of doing things? Or perhaps it was that the threats were issued in French? It appeared that, whatever documentation they required, and however much we could show them the correct paperwork, the negotiations were really about how much they should be 'paid' for letting us progress. Mobutu's legacy was corruption from the top to the bottom of society.

On site I was able to view the core that had been drilled, laid out and labelled neatly in boxes ready to be shipped overseas for analysis. Though most was grey rock, parts glimmered and glittered with the ore and minerals that infused the land. The prime aim was to identify copper. Within the rock this showed as green: the malachite that was carved and sculpted to make many trinkets sold in Zambian markets. Finding copper was not difficult in this area, but they needed to be confident that there would be a high enough percentage to justify the costs of mining.

I enjoyed visiting the exploration sites as part of my job. They were always well organised, and the food was of excellent. I suspect I got a good deal, though, as standards tend to improve when the Head Office visits. I'd seen enough of their expense chits back in the accounts department to know that the diet varied little from day to day, with chicken and goat being the popular meats. My presence also threw them into a state of confusion as there was rarely a ladies' toilet. One site had built one specially for a visit by local dignitaries, but in Kolwezi I had to sing loudly and share the men's long drop.

I glanced at the toilet in the hotel room in Lubumbashi. I wasn't sure which was worse: that, or the primitive long drop. It was a moment to appreciate the comforts of home.

I'm looking forward to seeing you soon. Perhaps you will come and meet me at the airport when I return?

Then I remembered the inward flight from Ndola, and wondered if we'd have the same plane back. Most African airlines (certainly the ones connected to the DRC) were banned by European authorities due to their poor safety records. The planes we flew in were small: maybe fifteen seats in total, single seats on either side of the aisle. On the way there I had been just behind the right wing. It didn't give much of a view, other than of a big, white stretch of metal: sections studded together and the usual flaps to control take-off and landing. I had spent most of the journey north watching one particular rivet wibble and wobble, gradually working looser and looser, until, somewhere close to Chingola, it fell off. I wondered whether I should scream, or alert someone to our impending doom, but presumably the other half-dozen along the strip were more than adequate to hold the wing together as we didn't plummet to destruction. I consoled myself with the presumption that pre-flight checks would notice the missing bolt and replace it before the plane returned to the air.

I miss you both, and Daddy. See you soon!
Love,
Mummy

I folded the sheet of paper and hid it inside a book in my luggage. If there was a postal system in Lubumbashi I was not aware of it. This letter would be handed over to the recipients in person, rather detracting from the glory of a missive from foreign parts. They, no doubt, would lose interest very quickly, take the letter and lose it amongst toys and books in their bedroom. But I knew I'd written it, and the love it sent to them, and one day – maybe one day – they'd appreciate just how much their mother missed them.

But, on boarding the plane, I wondered whether they would ever receive it, as I noticed a bolt ominously still missing from the right wing.

PROBLEMS ON THE PLOT

"You've been a long time," I said, as Stephen came through the back door, cockroach sprayer slung over his right arm. "Could have sworn you did the bit by my study nearly an hour ago."

Putting the chemicals safely away under the sink, he went to wash his hands and arms in the utility room. "Yes, well, I got side-tracked when I went to spray round Precious' home."

"Oh? What happened?"

"Precious told me the toilet was smelling." All of a sudden I was grateful that he was washing his hands thoroughly, and not doing so in the kitchen. "She said she told Henry."

Stephen looked at me sceptically. Maybe she did, but neither of them mentioned it to me.

"I don't know why she thought Henry could solve

it," Stephen continued. "He probably doesn't feel that he could or should take orders from her. And, to be honest, I can only imagine him looking at her and saying, 'Yes, Madam,' repeatedly while nodding his head."

I giggled. No-one ever knew if their message had properly sunk in with Henry.

"Anyway, foolishly I went to investigate."

Precious was right: the toilet did smell. In fact, it reeked and Stephen could almost follow the line of the drainage with his nose. Lifting a manhole cover a few metres from the house he located the problem: a mountain of rubbish clogging the pipework.

"It appears our staff use newspaper, which doesn't have the same flushability as toilet paper," said Stephen. "Nor do socks or rocks or whatever else they attempted to dispose of."

He wiped his hands on a towel before continuing. "Henry helped me lift the manhole cover so I told him what to do to clear the problem. After standing there for five minutes watching him get nowhere I gave in and did it myself."

I grimaced.

He looked down at the towel and at his hands, then gave them a non-too subtle sniff. "I think I'll have a shower," he said.

While I made us both a cup of tea, I thought about this incident a little more. I couldn't help suspecting it was simply going to happen again within another couple of months, so either Henry was going to have to get himself dirty (clearly not high on his agenda), our staff needed to change their toilet habits or we would have to have another scheme.

Fresh from his shower I tackled Stephen.

"I can't see how it's going to change," I said.

"I know. It's not necessarily Precious' fault – or

rather, the fault of the residents. Precious pointed out that the gardeners also use the toilet in the servants' quarters."

"They'll all be blaming each other, no doubt."

"Exactly," said Stephen. "Maybe that's why Henry didn't want to be involved? He didn't want to concede any liability?"

"I'm quite prepared to make Precious and her family responsible for clearing the drain if the gardeners aren't using it," I said.

Stephen drank his tea, obviously thinking hard. No doubt he never wanted to deal with that mess again. Eventually he said, "What we need is a long drop."

"A long drop?"

"Yes, an outside, self-composting toilet."

"I know what it is," I said crossly. "I've used one more recently than you, I bet. I was just wondering if there were rules and regulations regarding them."

"You're the one who should know," he said. Then, to my blank face: "Well, from work – the water divination department."

"Oh yes!" One section of the company I worked for specialised in locating suitable places to drill for water. Though they didn't use forked sticks we still teased them about their divining powers. In reality, their assessments were based on geography (seeing where streams were flowing above ground) and geology (knowing the type of rock). Their skills were in high demand, as a well that produced a steady flow of water could multiply exponentially the crop output on parched arable land. "I'll ask on Monday. Assuming there's no restrictions, what do you propose?"

"There's a lot of space at the bottom of the plot. Dig a big hole – Henry and Calvin can do that – and then I guess we'd need some sort of topping off."

I rescued his uncertainty. "Another work question.

They dig long drops all the time for the mineral exploration camps."

It was yet another unexpected learning curve that Zambia threw at me: toilet creation. Two years after arriving in this astonishing country, I took it all in my stride. After all, who doesn't design and build a long drop? How my life had changed.

∾

Stephen had just returned with his third load of cement and stones. The long drop had been dug and now Calvin was in charge of constructing a safe, solid standing area above it. For a small circle it required a lot of cement and The Bishop was converted into a transit van for the day.

"What's up with Mace?" Stephen asked. The kittens were usually very quiet and placid and, despite being with us for over a month, rarely left their basket outside the back door. Yet Mace was in a frenzy, out of his basket and buzzing around the garage, yowling his little head off. There was no obvious reason, until I went to investigate his basket.

Nutmeg wasn't there.

To have one kitten prowling around was unexpected; but to have the other missing was incomprehensible, even if it explained Mace's wild behaviour.

We hunted high and low. No-one had seen either of the kittens venture more than a metre or two from their basket before, so we were all astonished by Nutmeg's disappearance. Precious and Sherry were sent to scour the house, and Calvin was roped into the search party in the garden. Matthew tried, in vain, to hold and console Mace, receiving a vicious scratch on his arm for the effort.

But Nutmeg was nowhere to be found. Mace was

unsettled for days, but it turned out that Nutmeg was gone for good.

∻

"Stephen, Eleanor has an almighty spot on her stomach. Can you come and have a look?"

I'd been watching the pustule grow over the last few days, expecting it to pop or deflate, and had finally come to the conclusion something wasn't quite right. Eleanor was totally unbothered by it, and it was only when dressing or undressing her that I noticed.

Stephen stood behind me and looked over my shoulder. He frowned, and asked me to move out of the way. On closer examination he concluded, "I think it's a putze fly."

"Putze?" I repeated, then remembered. "Oh, putzes! Flies that lay eggs in our washing, and are the reason we iron everything so that they don't burrow into our skin and – eurgh!"

I stopped short. This was my daughter: my beautiful two-year-old girl. And right now she had a maggot growing inside her.

"Does she need to see a doctor?" I asked.

Stephen turned and stared at me. "What do you think I am?" he asked.

Not all moments in one's marriage are excellent. Meekly, I apologised. In a softer tone he said, "Do we have some Vaseline? We need to smother the spot in that first."

I rushed off to search the bathroom cabinet. Successful, I returned with the jar and Stephen smeared a large dollop onto Eleanor's belly. She, meanwhile, was happily chattering away to herself. I sat down on the bed next to her, assuming I'd need to distract her by waving dolly in front of her face.

"How long does she have to be like this?"

"I don't know. About an hour?"

"An hour? How are we going to keep her entertained that long?" I was anxious about her nudity too, as we hadn't started potty training and I had no confidence that, set free from nappies, she would last an hour without an accident.

"Oh, just let her run around for a bit," Stephen said, and disappeared back to the study.

It was clearly not going to be an early bedtime for Eleanor. I put a video on and prayed that she wouldn't make a mess on the sofa.

I struggled to last the full sixty minutes before asking Stephen if it was time to look at the growth again.

"Hmmm, yes," he said thoughtfully, before heading in the opposite direction. I took him at his word, rather than his action, and picked up Eleanor and lay her back down on her bed. Stephen reappeared carrying some tissue, a torch and a pair of tweezers.

"Now then," he said, "let's see." I held Eleanor, stroking her forehead, trying to keep her still and calm her down. He pointed the torch at her stomach and murmured, "Yes, yes…" and then, "I think I can see it."

Straightening up he said, "Right, let's see if we can get it out. You OK Eleanor?"

Eleanor stuck her arm in her mouth and nodded furiously.

"Good! Keep as still as you can, please."

More furious nodding.

Stephen turned to me. "Can you hold the torch?"

"Sure!" I said. Eleanor was quite placid now, a combination of end-of-day exhaustion and her father's words.

Stephen took the tweezers and delved into the Vaseline. A second later he pulled hard, and out came a maggot.

It was about two centimetres long, white, with Michelin-man style rings and beady black eyes. This creature had lived parasitically on Eleanor's stomach for the last couple of weeks. I felt nauseated. It was the most revolting thing to see come out of my daughter.

She barely whimpered. I let Stephen dispose of the creature while I wiped the grease from Eleanor's tummy and placed a large plaster over the affected area.

I had hoped that was the end of it but a week or two later there was another spot on Eleanor, and a week after that I had one. The worst appeared on the back of my hand, which I had assumed was a standard spot. When it became quite inflamed I went to see the local doctor, expecting him to prescribe antibiotics, but he said it was a putze fly. I queried this, given that the back of my hand had very little contact with fly-egg-infested clothes.

"I've seen them everywhere," he declared, which made my mind boggle.

In one of the most excruciatingly painful experiences in my life, two nurses spent quarter of an hour squeezing and pressing the thin skin near my knuckles to extract the pus and habitat that was nurturing the maggot. I never did see the creature emerge (it was certainly not of the size of Eleanor's first friend) but they stopped savaging me when there was more blood than other discharge. I had neither fainted nor screamed, though both were a near thing.

I questioned Precious, who did most of the ironing, and she said that the iron was not working well. "It doesn't get hot," she said. I saw this as a fundamental flaw and straightaway bought a replacement.

༧

We'd reached August and there had been no rain since

April. The grass was brown and the wind whipped up dust. Sipping my cup of tea on the terrace I looked out over the swathe of beige my garden had become. Not much to be proud of. I decided we really needed a sprinkler rotation system if we were to have any grass for my children to play on.

I called out to Henry. "Please can you get the sprinkler out and water the grass?"

"Yes, Madam."

An hour later I returned to find Henry standing in the middle of the lawn holding the hose and squirting the output over a tiny area. Clearly the idea of a sprinkler had no meaning to him. Ungenerously, I wondered what had happened to the third replacement sprinkler I'd purchased since moving but was relieved, after a little investigation, to find it under a pile of hosing in the garage.

I took it round the front to Henry. There was water pouring from the outside tap that stood proud underneath our water tower. It ran down the attached hose and formed a small pond underneath. I wanted to scream. *Why don't you use the proper attachments rather than just jamming the hose onto the tap?* I held back my anger and decided to teach Henry about the sprinkler first. Stephen could sort out the tap later.

"Henry!"

"Yes, Madam."

"You need to use this." I could see confusion spread across his face. But my Zambian employees rarely admitted to being ignorant of something, or being out of their depth. He quickly masked his feelings with a broad smile and took the sprinkler, turning it over and over in his hands.

"Here," I said, "if we attach it to the hose here..." I pointed at the hose end. "Then the water pushes it round and round, spreading out over the grass."

"Oh, yes Madam."

I wished his words filled me with confidence. "Go and switch off the tap and we'll give it a try."

Henry did as he was told (this was a task I was confident he could complete). Together we jammed the sprinkler on the far end of the hose before Henry switched the tap on again. Miraculously it worked. I was not sure which of us was more surprised. We stood and admired the swirling water, spreading across a few square metres of lawn. As I watched the dainty drops fall, I realised that this was not going to get us very far, very fast.

"You must move it around every fifteen minutes or so," I said, but even this, I realised, would barely cover our vast lawn in a day. The far side was going to have to be abandoned to nature. I left Henry, smile still fixed across his face, and returned to my desk. My quick tea-break had taken over an hour. Some days a seemingly simple task could take an age in Zambia.

FUELLING MY FEARS

I was perfecting the great British art of queuing. Known for our patience, lining up in an orderly fashion and tutting at those who dare to push in, I was emulating my countrymen by waiting for fuel. The Bishop and I were static on the main Great East Road behind about a dozen cars waiting to get into the service station. The ones at the front moved on every few minutes, a rotation rate that gave confidence that fuel was available.

Despite Zambia being landlocked, fuel supply was not normally a problem. An arterial oil pipe had been built in the 1970s, which enabled fuel to reach the country almost directly from tankers on the Indian Ocean. Zambia had its own refinery and a decent enough road network to transport it to the main towns throughout the country. However, the oil had run out, apparently because they had shut down the Indeni Refinery for a few weeks for urgent repairs. Inexplicably, for two days the general public were unaware of this. But then fuel became unavailable and the queues began. Forecourt prices nearly doubled overnight, as all the fuel had to be brought in by road using tankers.

I edged The Bishop forward a couple of spaces.

The hyper-inflationary fuel issue of the last couple of weeks was not helped by the wider economic picture. Every so often Stephen and I would assess our financial situation. Paid in sterling, our battle when we first arrived was to divide the kwacha amount by 7500. As time had passed the kwacha had weakened, so dividing first by 8000 and latterly by over 9000 was easier. I was longing for it to reach 10000K to £1 so the maths would be simple.

The finances were further complicated by the US dollar, the hard currency of desire around which calculations were usually based. It had risen to over 5000K to $1 (another fairly easy sum) but suddenly strange things were happening to the Zambian economy. Almost overnight, the rate dropped to 3200K to $1, with a proportional fall against the British pound.

Stephen wanted to completely understand the situation and felt that I, as an accountant, ought to be able to explain it. As I queued in the car I went over in my head the conversation we'd had earlier, wondering if my calculations were correct.

"So, let me get this straight," he'd said, "if we, the UK, have 3% inflation and Zambia has 20% inflation, in a world where everything was logical and fair the kwacha would rise against the pound? Is that the basis for variable exchange rates?"

Stephen had pushed my knowledge of macroeconomics close to its limits. I'd had to do some quick calculations on a scrap of paper before I confirmed.

"I think so. After one year an identical item would be worth an increased amount of kwacha and sterling, but more so kwacha, and so the exchange rate increases."

"But it isn't what's happening at the moment."

"Well, it has done in the past." I had defended this argument with reference to the previous two years and a lot of squiggles on my sheet of paper.

"So why has it suddenly dropped? Inflation is still higher here than in the UK, but the exchange rate's falling."

I'd put my pen down. "That, I'm afraid, I don't know."

Rumours abounded as to why the kwacha had so suddenly strengthened against the dollar, most of which were unflattering to those in power. It coincided with the G8 writing off the country's debt, and I wondered whether those rich world leaders had anticipated this consequence. Expats reliant on income from overseas had, in effect, suffered a 30% cut in income. Some were considering leaving, but most of our friends were prepared to battle it out. And to the ordinary Zambian, who didn't have the luxury of foreign coinage, it made little short-term difference.

The opportune call from a friend to say that there was fuel at Manda Hill had relieved me of further highfalutin finance discussion. *A mixed blessing*, I thought, as I edged forwards another couple of spaces.

On another occasion I might not have made the mad dash to queue for fuel, but we had booked to go away for a weekend. At the end of August Stephen was due to go back to the UK for about five weeks to attend two international conferences, as well as to catch up with his supervisors. I was hoping that the spare time on his own would enable him to write half his PhD before he returned to complete his six-month extension. The sooner the PhD was completed, the sooner he could apply for the second level of grants and funding, which was imperative if we were to stay long term in Zambia. In my mind it was all so straightforward.

Given we would be apart for over a month, we had planned a family weekend break. In reality, I was less worried about the fuel crisis than the holiday. This time we weren't staying in a lovely, safe lodge: instead, we were camping. Stephen had bought two small tents from friends who were leaving and was keen to try them out, together with our fledgling camping equipment. I had none of his confidence. The tents didn't seem to provide much protection. I was reminded of the story a friend had told me before we left the UK. His daughter had travelled to Africa and camped under a tree. During the night there had been an awful rumpus going on, and she had woken in the morning to discover she'd been sleeping underneath the elephants' favourite acacia tree. Not an experience I wanted to repeat with two young children in tow.

Inching forwards, I was nearly off the main road and onto the forecourt.

Thankfully, Gwyn and Gareth were due back from the UK before Stephen left and I couldn't wait. I hadn't realised just how much I enjoyed their company and relied on them being around. I was missing their evening visits: mainly the wine drunk with Gwyn while Gareth played with the children in the swimming pool. He'd throw Matthew from a great height and encourage Eleanor to doggy paddle in her armbands; a gloriously light-hearted way to end a day.

I couldn't believe it was a year since Gwyn had arrived in the country, she was such a regular part of our lives. I wondered how Gareth was getting on with my in-laws. I had little doubt that he had easily won them over, but I'd picked up on a little anxiety before they'd left. It reminded me of my first terrifying visit to Stephen's parents. Would they like me? Would I like them? At the time I was uncertain whether there was a future in my own relationship with Stephen, which made it all the more difficult to establish friendships with his family.

But Grannie and Grampa were the easiest people in the world, delightfully welcoming and never allowing an uncomfortable moment. I wondered – just wondered – if Gareth would pop the question while he was there. Or at least ask permission to do so: my guess was that he'd do everything in a very traditional, and romantic, way. I sighed. *It had only been eight months: was it just wishful thinking?*

I edged forward towards the pumps: only three cars ahead of me now.

The other gap in our lives was Sherry. Her mother had fallen ill a couple of weeks earlier and died within a few days. It was heart-breaking to see the Sherry we knew and loved, who was perpetually smiley and jokey with the children, brought low by grief. The loss of a mother was perhaps the only thing I could truly empathise about with Sherry, and it filled me with sorrow to see her so upset. She had gone to the village for the burial and I hoped she would be back before term started again.

Mulling these things over, I wondered: *why did I want to stay in this country?* I seemed to be leaping from one crisis to the next. No fuel. Poor exchange rate. No full-time maid.

Thankfully term was soon to begin again, and my eldest child would enter his reception year at 'big school'. It was a shame Stephen would be away and miss his first day. Eleanor, now approaching three years old, was also moving up a class: the tiny baby I had brought to Zambia was growing into a fine, feisty young girl.

At long last, I reached the pump. The attendant dutifully removed the cap and filled The Bishop with diesel. I watched carefully as there were stories of them not starting at zero, thus creaming off the top a little cash for themselves. No such worries today: I was finished and rushed home for some lunch. A full tank, and our mini-holiday was back on.

The lodge was further down the dusty track than we had expected, past a small village of mud huts roofed with straw and the inevitable clutch of chickens pecking around in the dirt. We didn't run over any, although it was a close thing.

We arrived later than planned, of course, but to our surprise long before sunset. Not that this helped much, as it took the novice campers nearly three hours to set up the tents and associated paraphernalia. This lodge site offered it all: camp site, luxury tents, a handful of rondavals with en suites and even a self-catering chalet. It was on the banks of the Zambezi, in the stretch between the Kariba Dam and the Lower Zambezi National Park. We were reliably informed that the park was one of the best in the country for viewing animals, as they were trapped between the hills of the escarpment and the deep flowing river. I was looking forward to the chance to explore there. On the other side of the river was Zimbabwe.

Our long weekend covered Stephen's birthday (a number divisible by two, but otherwise unremarkable) and we had planned a ride on the motorboat down to the park area as a special treat. For now, we had lit a fire in the boma outside our tents and Stephen and I were drinking a glass of wine before bed. Though the day had been warm, it was cooling off rapidly.

There was a yelp from one of the tents. I sighed, threw back my head and looked up at the stars.

"I can still hear them," I said.

There was an awkward moment when I knew I ought to have put down my wine and gone to tell my children one last time to settle down, be quiet and go to sleep; but selfishness and exhaustion took hold. I wanted to stay where I was and enjoy my drink in peace.

"I'll go," said Stephen, heaving himself out of his chair.

Great: now I have guilt as well.

I pulled myself into a sitting position. *If not a good mother then I must be a good wife.* I topped up Stephen's glass of wine.

"All quiet?" I asked when he rejoined me.

"There are threats greater than Damocles' sword if I hear another squeak out of them," he said, with a large swig of his wine. "Gosh! It's nice out here!"

"Beautiful and calm. And safe. Boy! I didn't think that earlier! That creature was something else," I said. "It was so big and just – there! No distance at all from us."

An involuntary shudder ran down my back. Along the side of our camping pitch was a small, bushy dip in the land, where presumably a stream ran during the height of the rainy season, and then a communal area for the campers. We were the only people here so had exclusive use of the toilet and shower block, built bush-camp style: all wooden, windowless and with a modicum of thatched roofing. The shower, however, was open to the skies. When the sun was up, there was a wonderful romance to it; but as night fell, the chill in the air stole the romance that a starlit shower should have brought. August nights still held a gasp of winter.

It was as we were putting up the tents earlier that I had heard something move in the bushes.

"Kids, come here!" I called, halting their japes. I grabbed their hands and held them tight as a creature lumbered out of the bushes and onto the path. Stephen stopped hammering in the tent pegs and watched with us.

"Mummy, what is it?" Matthew asked.

"Sshh!" I hissed. "I think its a baby crocodile."

The crocodile was between us and the toilet block. It was slime-green and scaly, eyes either side of his head above his long, flat snout. Short, stumpy legs with distinct fingers propelled him as he slithered across the grass and path, a striped tail curving behind.

We stood stock still and stared. I knew the best thing was to not move: movement would encourage it to chase us. What I didn't understand was why a crocodile was so far out of the water. How had it got up the bank? The steep drop at the water's edge concerned me for the children's safety when they ran around on the grass, but I had thought it was too much to make hippos and crocodiles a real danger.

I was clearly wrong.

Slowly it made its way across the path and into the bushes between us and the river. When it was out of sight we began talking again in low voices.

"Has it gone?" I asked.

"I think so," said Stephen.

"Is it safe to go down the path?"

"I don't know. Why didn't the crocodile come for us?"

"Too far from the water, I think. They don't attack on land as a rule. I think they like to drag their prey under the water."

"Mummy, I need a wee!"

I looked at Matthew. The toilets were the other side of the crocodile.

"OK!" I said in a bright, falsely cheerful voice. "Let's see if we can get there via the car park."

I took a firm hold of him with one hand and Eleanor with the other and, with one last backward glance, we walked away. I swear the leaves of the bush twitched.

Stephen joined us at the toilets before we'd finished.

"I thought I'd come and reassure you that the creature's gone," he said.

"Really?" I said incredulously.

"Really," he repeated with certainty. "I saw it follow the line of the bushes down stream and then into the river."

Nevertheless, I had let Stephen walk in front of us as we crossed the same piece of path back to the tents, just in case.

Now, sat around a camp fire, stars twinkling in the sky, I wondered how safe we really were. Stephen had picked up our African Animals reference book and was flicking through it by torchlight.

"I don't think it was a crocodile," he said eventually. "I think it was this."

He passed the book and headlamp, pointing at a photo that looked like a crocodile. It also looked like what we had seen. I read the description.

"A Monitor Lizard?" Looking at the picture closely, I could see it didn't have the size of head of a crocodile: it was narrower somehow, less protuberant eyes. In the calm of looking in a guidebook, it was much easier to recognise the different proportions of head, neck, legs and tail. There weren't any visible teeth in its lazy smile and, on reflection, its movement had been more serpentine than the silent, forward-motion of a crocodile.

I smiled. What fear could there be of a lizard, albeit one that was four foot long?

A comfortable silence ensued. The fire crackled in the pit and the cicadas trilled in the trees. In the distance a hippo grunted: a loud snort followed by a splash of water. I breathed in the aroma of burning wood and fresh greenery.

Here it was difficult to imagine the war and famine that plagued Africa. We'd left behind a city anxious about its fuel supply and the state of the economy. It was hard to believe that there were troubles just across the water and that Zimbabwe was now a place of unrest. Why was man so intent on killing animals, the planet, even themselves?

In this place and moment, all was at peace with the world.

∂

Eleanor wailed again.

Just whose blinking stupid idea was it to go camping?

I was freezing. I thought my feet were turning into ice blocks. *Is it possible to get frostbite in Zambia?* I regretted not getting a double sleeping bag that I could have shared with Stephen.

He was over the moon to be sleeping outdoors, delighted to be the intrepid explorer. Or at least he would have been, if he were awake. His ability to sleep soundly through every noise either of our children made was one of the most frustrating and threatening parts of our marriage.

My sole consolation was that I had manipulated the situation so that he was next to the tent door. It might require a lot of pushing and shoving, but *he* was the one who was going to have to deal with Eleanor.

"Stephen!" I called, poking him hard with my elbow. "Eleanor's awake again."

Wearily he woke. "Ellie, stop crying," he said.

There was a moment's silence before she started again.

"Eleanor, lie down and go to sleep."

"Stephen, that's not going to work," I hissed. "You'll have to help her."

Begrudgingly he extracted himself from his sleeping bag and unzipped our tent. He crawled the two metres over to the kids' identical tent, unzipped it and sorted her out, before returning.

"She'd crawled out of her sleeping bag."

"Again?"

Eleanor was in an adult sleeping bag that we'd borrowed. Never the best at sleeping, I assumed she'd woken and decided to play. Crawling out of a bag that was too big for her she must have got cold and in the darkness couldn't see to get back into it again.

"What did you do?"

"Put her back inside the sleeping bag and told her to go back to sleep." Stephen rolled over.

"Thank you," I whispered to his already drowsy body. I tried to mould myself against him for warmth but the principal lesson I learnt was that I really relished warm nights. Camping in Zambia in early August was noted as being too cold.

In the morning I woke early. Although my feet were finally warm, my nose felt it was still too chilly to venture out, so I persuaded Stephen that getting up and making me a mug of tea would be a great idea. Thankfully he was still full of the joys of camping, so this was not too difficult. He rose to greet the new day and rapidly got the fire lit and kettle boiling. I wriggled deeper into my sleeping bag as fresh morning air rushed in through the tent door.

When Stephen came back with the mugs he whispered fiercely. "Catharine! Catharine! Quick – look!"

"Do I have to? Now?" I groaned.

"Sshh! Yes, yes – now…"

He disappeared outside. I shuffled to the door of the tent, still cocooned in my sleeping bag. Leaning out, my eyes followed where Stephen was pointing. In the bushes no more than ten metres away, was a bushbuck. A reddish-brown colour, with distinctive white stripes and spots across his belly, this antelope likes to live in woodland and forests, as his name suggests. Our visitor was nibbling on some leaves, but after a minute or so became aware of our presence and shot back into the undergrowth.

"Wow! I don't think I've ever been so close to an antelope!" I exhaled. "He was beautiful!"

"He certainly was."

We sat in companionable silence for a few moments, cradling our teas. I listened hard, as we had been taught by previous guides. There was the faint sound of Eleanor snoring as she struggled to breathe through her blocked nose, and the louder rumblings of the river tumbling over boulders towards its destination. Then – far in the distance – I could hear a lion roar.

"Did you hear that?"

"The lion? Yes. Not too close, I hope."

"It sounded quite distant."

I smiled, loving the peace and being so close to nature. This was the delight of bush camping and almost made up for being frozen overnight. Besides, I was comforted by the potential luxury that would make this camping experience bearable: at any time, I could get a decent cup of tea at the lodge next door.

Later, when I'd confidently walked the path to and

from the toilet block a few times, it struck me that those roaring lions had been prowling around the area all night. *Had the lions thought 'time for lunch' when they'd heard Eleanor cry in the night? And how safe had my husband been, crawling between the tents?* Two tents were perhaps not the safest option.

LIONS, OR TIGERS?

"Whee!" I exclaimed, as we sped down the river.

Matthew and Eleanor were grinning from ear to ear. A speedboat was a further adventure for my little African explorers, and a lot more exciting than the usual offer of a canoe. As so many times before, I wondered what the British government would think of me now. I was probably the ultimate in irresponsible parenting. Neither child had a lifejacket. There were crocodiles in this river, and hippos, and other creatures that would love to eat them for lunch. Yet they sat still – one next to Stephen, one next to me – and peered excitedly over the edge of the boat.

The boat had plenty of room for us all, so we could move around freely. We slowed down as our driver and guide looked out for wildlife. Stephen grabbed his binoculars; I hung onto my sunhat. The children giggled mischievously as the water rushed past the bow of the boat.

The driver cut the engine. "Puku," he said, pointing. He waited while we located them on the river bank, their sleek russet-brown bodies camouflaged in the surrounding bush and dust. Sure enough, there were a couple of antelope looking intently at us. We had seen many a puku before, but once again I marvelled at the guide's ability to spot them among the scrub while sailing past so quickly.

The journey calmed down a little after that. We heard the soft *whoosh-plop!* of crocodile slipping into the water as we approached. We saw the fish eagle hovering above: watching, waiting, swooping down… then back to its perch high in the treetops.

The driver cut the engine, letting the boat gently drift with the current as he showed us the Zimbabwean bank. Here, in the many holes made in the sandy wall, were hundreds of bee-eaters: green, blue, yellow, splashes of red. The bright colours sparkled in the sunshine, contrasting with the pale background. They appeared unperturbed by us. We spoke in hushed whispers, in awe at the brilliance of their display.

I could probably have stayed and watched them all day, but the children grew restless. Given their ages it was hardly surprising. Besides, I wanted to see elephant. We moved on at speed.

The river was amazing. It was wide, scattered with little islands and sandbanks. We moved away from the Zimbabwean side (the guide muttered something about not being allowed there, which made me wonder why we were there earlier) and sailed on past various other lodges on the Zambian side. We spotted one we had stayed in two years earlier, shortly after arriving in Zambia. It brought back wonderful memories, and also a flush of embarrassment as I thought how innocent and naïve we must have appeared then.

The riverbank was dotted with houses. We passed the odd local fisherman in his dugout canoe, threading his line with bait. Our driver greeted them all in local tongue, clearly by name, and we smiled and waved politely. On seeing Eleanor's blonde hair, big grin and podgy arms, one in particular returned a wide smile: white teeth against dark skin, accentuating the missing ivories; a wrinkly, weathered face acknowledging the beauty and innocence of young life.

Our driver cut the engine again. "Elephant!" he said, pointing up on top of the bank.

Sure enough, brazenly walking through a group of mud huts was a family of elephants. We knew by the standard of hut construction, the spacing around them and the inclusion of a larger building further downstream that this was another lodge, not a local village. I recalled our holiday at Mfuwe, when I had been trapped in our chalet with the children while a herd of eight elephants ate the trees around it. Eventually we had been rescued by one of the guides, who had spotted our predicament while out on a game drive the other side of a pond. The image of elephants immediately outside the window round the bath, close enough to touch, was one I'd never forget.

I wondered whether there was anyone in the riverbank huts or whether they'd all gone out on a game drive, expecting to see animals from the back of a jeep little realising they'd have seen more by staying at home – certainly had a wilder experience.

The elephants weren't doing much and, being high up on the bank, were not great entertainment. I'd ticked my box, so we moved on, hoping to see more downstream. We passed some harrumphing hippos; saw a shoebill stork in flight. The morning was warming up but the laziness of messing around in a boat was delightfully gentle and soporific. The animals weren't daft. In the National Park they were properly protected, so there they would stay if possible. Here, to the west, was a Game Management Area. This meant they were looked out for, but there were not such stringent rules against poaching. More pertinently, they were also sensible enough to stay in the shade as the sun got hotter. Our chances of seeing animals were fast diminishing.

A gap opened up in the riverbank on our left. As we got closer it became apparent that this was more than a little tributary: it was a full river, flowing into the Zambezi. Our driver slowed the boat, I assumed in order to negotiate the rapid and uncertain strength of water flow when two rivers join, but then he turned the boat, headed slightly up the river and pulled over to the left hand bank.

"It must be the Chongwe river," said Stephen to me. He turned to the driver. "Chongwe?"

"Yes," he said, indicating upstream. "That is the National Park." He pointed at the land on the other side of this river: the Lower Zambezi National Park.

It was the reason I had been excited by this boat trip. Now was our chance to see the multitude of animals that allegedly lived there. Even in the heat of the day, we could expect to see the animals and their young coming down for a drink.

"We are carrying on down there?" I asked, pointing to the continuation of the Zambezi.

"We stop," said the driver. He pulled out the cool box, ready to offer us all a drink.

"I know we're stopped, but we're going on past the park?"

"No, we stop here. Mosi? Fanta? Coke?"

"Why are we not going on?"

"We can't. We stop here."

I had to give up my dream of going further. This stop was a break from the sun, to rehydrate and to have the chance of seeing a few animals; but from the wrong side of the river that creates the western border of the park. Our downstream journey ended, but our guide was unable to give a satisfactory explanation. Time? Regulations? Perhaps speedboats weren't allowed on the next stretch of river? Whatever the reason, we had to make do with the rather boring stretch of water we had already travelled.

Pulling up to the river bank did mean we could get out and stretch our legs. It wasn't much: we were resting on a sandy bank that a crocodile might occupy: to sunbathe, before he took a quick dip in the cool river waters. Still, the children got to scramble up the bank a little and Matthew was delighted to be allowed a Coke (a birthday treat).

Time moved on, and so did we. We clambered back into the boat and prepared for our journey back upstream. To our surprise, after a few minutes of enthralling speed, the boat slowed again and our driver offered us fishing rods.

Before starting out we had been given the option of a fishing trip and had refused. The vegetarian in me was not happy about fishing. Hooking creatures in their mouths, no doubt causing physical damage before pulling them from the water to thrash about, resulting either in death (just about permissible) or being returned to the water, all felt repugnant to me. Surely returning them, although potentially offering life, cannot be offering the life they had before their mouths were gouged?

No, fishing was not for me, so we had chosen a boat trip to view animals instead.

But, in the circumstances it would have been churlish to refuse a Zambian offering fishing rods.

Besides, we were utterly at his mercy given he was in control of the boat. There were four rods, so Stephen, Matthew and I took one each, with one for the driver. He hooked some bait and taught us how to throw a line.

The lines were sized for adults, so Matthew struggled. He also didn't understand why nothing took the bait immediately. Eleanor was engrossed in a book in the belly of the boat. Due to our proximity, it fell to me to help Matthew. Reluctantly I held onto the rod, hoping that I would be able to detect a bite to make him happy.

Nothing happened.

The children grew tetchy and, despite a repeat attempt, throwing lines the other side and drifting silently, there were no takers.

The driver started the engine and drove on. We could tell he wasn't happy. He muttered about the fishing and decided that the bait was the problem. Presumably the worms were dead, or something. He spied one of the local fishermen and went over for a chat. We couldn't follow the exact conversation but watched as he negotiated to buy some fresh bait from the old man. Purchases made, he restarted the engine and we drove off, waving to the fisherman.

"We try again," said the driver.

I was not sure of the wisdom of this. I was still uncomfortable about the concept of fishing and the children were bored. We wanted to see animals. *A lion would be good (from the safety of the boat…).*

Nevertheless, we decided to give it one last go. The new bait might make all the difference and, while we probably couldn't entertain them for long, the children were being remarkably well behaved. Unfortunately, Matthew's patience ended: his newly-baited rod was shoved into my hands and mine was redundant.

I'll just sit and hold it I thought.

Engine off, we sat in the peace, holding our rods, gently floating down the river. Allegedly the Zambezi was teaming with fish, but again there was no bite. At one point Stephen wondered if he had caught something, but reeling in the line revealed nothing but a hook. Maybe something bit and got away; maybe it just got caught up in the reeds.

The driver revved the engine again and we went back upstream a few hundred yards, before being left to drift again. Having no real responsibility I began to quite enjoy myself. I simply had to sit holding a rod while I kept an eye on the riverbanks for lions. Matthew had moved along inside the boat and showed occasional interest in what was going on with his father's rod, but I was at the other end and left out of their conversations. Sunglasses on, I was at rest in a little world of my own. *If this is all fishing involved I could get used to it.* There was a small tug on my line, but we had drifted into the reeds again so I assumed it was caught in some grass.

I looked at the driver. He must have noticed something, for he nodded at me.

"Should I reel it in?" I asked.

"No, leave it," he said.

A few more minutes and still no fish were caught. The boat had drifted a long way into the reeds and the driver decided it was time to move on. He started the engine and gently moved out. Stephen had already given up and was reeling in his line.

My line tugged again, and became taut. I glanced at the driver. He knew something was there. I interpreted his signals to mean I must reel in the line – carefully.

Slowly I wound it up. After a few turns it became apparent I had something bigger than a minnow on the end. This was going to be a battle.

I stood up to get better leverage. I walked the length

of the boat, dodging bodies along the way. Everyone was now interested in what I had caught.

"Keep going, Catharine!" I heard Stephen urging me on.

I wasn't sure how long I could hold out. It was a contest for supremacy.

"Gently, gently," said the guide. "Not too fast."

Too fast was unlikely. I was holding onto the rod for dear life. The tug at the other end was nearly enough to pull me in. *Could I have caught a crocodile?*

I discovered that there were times when the line was tight, and times when it was looser. When loose, I could reel the line in a bit. When tight I had to allow the fish to come to me. It was remarkable how quickly I could learn such things when it became a necessity: it was a choice between that and being pulled into the uncertain depths of the Zambezi river.

Suddenly, there it was: a massive fish splashing just below the water.

"What is it?" asked Matthew.

"A fish," said Stephen almost simultaneously with my, "I don't know!"

"Cor!" said Matthew, with all the astonishment and innocent enthusiasm of a four-year-old. It was too much of a struggle with the line for me to appreciate it.

"A tiger fish," corrected the guide. That I registered, and was taken aback. Tiger fish were the biggest fish in the rivers of Zambia. They got their name from their ferocious teeth, protruding slightly from their mouth, and stripes down the lengths of their backs. They were monstrous beasts.

I also knew they were the greatest game catch for a fisherman. Friends at church had spent whole weekends on rivers trying to catch one. People won competitions with these.

Mine was thrashing around, desperate to get away.

"OK, that's good," said the guide encouragingly. "Pull it in now."

I turned the handle, pulling the fish slightly out of the water, but it was too strong. I lost a bit of line, and the guide realised (then) that I needed help. He came to my side and gave extra support on the reeling, then left me at that end while he moved to take hold of the fish at the other. I was clinging on for dear life, as the fish flapped around in the air about five feet above the boat.

It was a whopper, fighting like mad. He unhooked it, being bitten in the process. He held its panting body in his arms, weighing it up. "About six, maybe six-and-a-half kilos," he said.

It was certainly huge, and now it was thrust into my arms so that the family could take a photo. They were all laughing. The vegetarian had caught the only catch of the day: one of the bigger tiger fish in the Zambezi.

Photos taken, the guide gently put the fish over the side. Tiger fish were expected to be 'catch and release' unless there was good reason, so it was set free again in the river.

I watched as it struggled to reacclimatise before it was off, fast as it could, weaving its way through the surface reeds, then lost in the depths of the river.

DROUGHT TOLERANCE

In Lusaka the dry season ran from April to October. Gradually the grass withered, turning brown from lack of water. All around town, gardeners were employed to spray and sprinkle to maintain an unnatural green. We were no exception.

On the Monday afternoon, after our weekend away, I found the sprinkler lying in the middle of the lawn, unused.

"Henry!"

He came running. "Yes, Madam?"

"Why isn't the sprinkler on?"

"No water, Madam."

"No water?"

"No, Madam."

"None at all?"

"No, Madam."

I was confused. Why didn't we have any water?

I went inside to ask Sherry and Precious if it was true. We turned on a kitchen tap. Water poured out, then splurted and stuttered, then stopped.

"No water," they said in unison.

"When did this happen?" I asked.

"After lunch?" Precious indicated with a shrug of her shoulders. They had obviously known for a while but hadn't thought it necessary to tell me.

"And the washing?"

Another shrug of the shoulders. Looking past Precious into the utility room I could see that it was still waiting to be done.

I was baffled, but knew there could be a million reasons for this information breakdown, probably all out of my control. I phoned my friend next door to ask if they had water.

"I think so. Wait a moment."

I heard her walk through to the kitchen, turn the tap and the sound of water flowing. No spluttering and gurgling. Hers was flowing freely.

"All fine here," she said.

"Oh, OK. I guess it's something peculiar to our system. I'll see what it's like in the morning."

"Well, call me if you need any help."

I put the phone down, but before I'd walked three metres it rang again.

"Only me!" she said. "I just thought: my water could be being pumped up from the borehole."

"Ah!" I said. "So there may be a problem with the mains supply." I looked at the clock, ticking towards 17 hours. "It's a bit late to get in touch with anyone at the water company now. I'll give them a ring in the morning."

"Sure. Sorry not to be more help."

A borehole! Why didn't we have one of those?

I thought it through. We would survive until the next day. The children could have a swim later, which for one night would substitute for a bath, and we'd enough filtered water for drinking. Hopefully everything would be sorted out overnight.

Thankfully, the next morning there was water. We all revelled in it flowing freely and I notched the previous day up to some blip in the system. But by the afternoon it had dried up again and on my return from work I was again caught with not having enough time to call the water company.

The following day I bought a couple of five-litre water bottles, stashing them away in the pantry as emergency supply. I spent a frustrating hour phoning the water company who were uninterested in my water supply. Having said that, my arguments seemed spurious, given we did have water in the morning. But shortly after lunch it ran out again. There was a lot of 'Yes, Madam', 'No, Madam' and 'We are sorry, Madam', but none of it got me anywhere. I asked if they could deliver some water to go in our storage tank, but apparently the relevant vehicle was not working. Once more we ended the day with a swim and bucket showers.

A week later and Stephen was fretting more than me as he was packing to leave for five weeks. The rumour was that one of the generators at the Kariba Dam was down for servicing, thus less water was in the system and the pressure had dropped. We lived on a barely perceptible hill but there was not enough water pressure during the day to pump it up and out of our taps.

However in the morning, before everyone got going, it was fine. We developed a routine (reliant on Sherry, of course). She arrived about an hour earlier than normal and started by filling the five-litre bottles with tap water. These were used sparingly during the day for drinking and washing. I was reminded of my travels with work to Kolwezi. There, a bucket resided next to the toilet for flushing: we adopted the same approach but, in the interests of water security, we only used it when absolutely necessary. We bathed in the swimming pool (or, better still, in a friend's) and Precious also changed her working hours to wash clothes in the morning while there was still some water pressure.

Stephen's worries even caused him to suffer a couple of sleepless nights just prior to leaving. He kept asking if I was all right, if I would manage, if I could cope. I loved the fact he was concerned, but our system was working reasonably well so I wasn't very worried. I reassured him that I had marvellous friends next door to whom I could turn if necessary, and the newspapers were reporting it would be fixed within a few days.

"Don't worry: I'll be fine!" I said.

When he left for the UK everything felt under control.

❧

In Stephen's absence there became less and less time during the working day when water was available. Our early morning bottling system still worked, but the worst part was I had no idea how long it would be until the service returned to normal. I gave up asking the water company and the papers were misinformed.

The smelliest problem was the swimming pool. The water level dropped so low that it couldn't be cleaned properly. Our neighbours devised a scheme, with the aid of a very long hose, for filling our pool with water pumped from their borehole. This rescued us from the pea soup that had formed and, to a large part, saved my sanity: the children could enjoy swimming again.

My friend Jenny's husband, Peter, had a man he was

trying to train to be a good plumber, and together they took on the project of fixing the system. They came round one weekend to assess the situation. We gazed up at the water tower. About ten metres above us, set on a sturdy metal frame, was a large white plastic container that held our water before it came into the house. Despite our attempts to look, there was no external evidence as to how much water it contained. Our conclusion (it was empty) was solely based on the knowledge we still had no water coming out of the taps.

"What can we do?" I asked, nervous of the answer.

Peter stroked his chin thoughtfully and looked around the base of the water tower. He switched on the tap at knee height and water flowed, weak but certain.

"I am confident that the water in here comes directly from the water company's supply. We can see the pipe coming down from the main road, parallel with the drive."

We could see a lot of our pipework. Everything had seemed very unclear at an earlier visit, so it was suggested we dig up some ground to locate the pipework and ascertain how it was flowing into the house. This had the added bonus of giving the gardeners something to do, since their usual job of watering the plants was impossible. They set about digging trenches across the lawn. Near the water tank there was no problem, as it was an unattractive and unused part of the plot. Henry began keenly digging up the tarmac across the drive until I rushed out to stop him, explaining that he didn't need to destroy that: he could just start on the grass the other side, where we expected the line of the pipe to come out. The front lawn now looked like a miniature battle scene, with trenches exposing pipes going to standpipes and junctions and even – thankfully – into the house.

Perhaps the most miraculous thing was the gardeners hadn't burst a pipe in the process. Then again, we had no water pressure, so how could I tell?

"Are you prepared to buy a water tank?" Peter asked.

"How much is it?" I asked.

"It's cheaper than the pump you'll require," he said, "but I think that's the answer. If we put a tank down here… then connect it with a pipe to here… then the water, which comes in here, can fill it first." He pointed at the appropriate junctions and continued with technical jargon. "There'll be a stopcock here, a ball like in a toilet to prevent overflow, but an overflow pipe if necessary. Here we'll need a two-way valve, here a non-reversing valve…"

I had switched off from the detail. "And that will mean we'll have water?"

If so, it was a deal.

꙳

He looked so grown up: a rucksack on his back, a small bag carrying a snack and a water bottle.

"Come on you! Let's take a photo."

"Mu-um, do we have to?"

"Yes," I said firmly. "We need to send it to Daddy."

Matthew's shoulders sank and he trudged out of the house behind me.

"Now then," I said, "how about here?" Sun behind me, plain white wall behind my boy but a bit of the garden to brighten it up: the perfect place for a snap.

Matthew stood obediently in position and, with a little persuasion, managed a smile as he squinted into the light.

"Excellent! Eleanor – do you want to be in the photo too?"

A bundle of blonde curls and ear to ear grin

bounded across the patio to join her brother. A couple more photos and we were done.

It was time to go. 'Big school' started today. Hand in hand we walked across the road, through the car park and up to the playground. Near the classroom door we met his teacher, and all the other mothers anxious about leaving their four-year-olds at the start of full-time education. I gave him a kiss goodbye, wishing Stephen was there to share the moment. Then, like pouring water into the ocean, he was away with his friends.

I watched him go, then turned for home.

For a couple of weeks, my days started with the arrival of Peter and his plumber. They planned what to buy and what to do in order that I could have water. At the completion of works I was given strict instructions not to use the pump if the water tank was empty, but otherwise the pump should give us enough pressure to have water in the house. Overnight and in the morning, when there was sufficient pressure from the mains supply, the tank would fill. When the pressure dropped during the day, I turned on the pump and (with a few restrictions to the hours when Precious could do the washing and a control-freak's paradise when the swimming pool was being filled) all worked well.

We had been over a month with negligible water but at last had developed a system that supplied enough for all our needs. Once more we could drink, ablute and swim freely. Furthermore, I had survived nearly four weeks without Stephen and all was fine.

More than survived, I reflected. *I'd lived!* I'd supervised the introduction of a better water system. I'd organised the staff when required (though they were largely self-regulating). The children had been marvellous and we'd settled into a routine of school and work. Gwyn was back from the UK and, together with my friends, I felt totally supported. I knew I had people I could turn to if I was in difficulty, or lonely, or bored, but best of all – I wasn't. Not that I didn't miss Stephen (he'd be back in a week and I couldn't wait!) but nothing had gone disastrously wrong.

I was relieved, considering our plans for the future. We anticipated that by February he'd be back in the UK, finishing his PhD while completing the professional requirements to become a consultant. Then he could apply for the next level of research funding and, all being well, a year on and he'd be back in Lusaka for a five-year project. We'd only be apart twelve months and, based on the one month I'd survived, I would cope. After all, I'd got through a month without water: surely it couldn't get any worse than that?

STEPHEN MISSES OUT

I stormed into the house, flung my bag down and headed straight to the kettle.

"What a waste of time that was!" I exclaimed.

Gwyn looked at me. "G&T?" she asked tentatively.

"That might be a better idea," I said, torn between the comfort of a cup of tea and alcohol. I took a deep breath and held it, before releasing it slowly. Gwyn was standing near the fridge, looking anxious. "Go on! I could have both! Would you like one too?"

"I might just do that," she replied.

Calming down a little I asked, "Is Gareth with the kids?"

"Yeah, they're having a ball in the pool. Not sure who's having most fun."

I paused to listen. I could hear splashing and squeals of laughter from the back of the house. "Better get him a drink too," I said, opening the glasses' cupboard.

Manoeuvring around the kitchen I was back on solid ground and Gwyn ventured to ask what had happened at school.

"Well," I said. "Miss M simply told me what I already know: Eleanor can't speak properly yet. She's following a similar pattern to Matthew and – let's face it – he's just won a house point for music, so talking late can't be too prejudicial to progress."

Gwyn snorted with laughter. I had learnt just the day before that Matthew had won his first house point and, given Stephen's complete lack of musical ability, I was delighted Matthew had inherited at least one positive trait from his mother.

Eleanor's language skills did concern us but we were reminded of stories of children who didn't speak at all until they were four years old and then came out with a complete sentence. Eleanor had a lot of words, albeit often poorly formed, and communicated well by pointing and flirting.

"What was Miss M talking about? Was there an additional point to the meeting?" Gwyn asked as we went through to the living room and sat down.

"I'm not entirely sure," I said. "She was very keen to say that Eleanor can't speak properly–"

"– Which you knew–"

"– and that she will be moving up into Miss P's class at half term –"

"– which you expected to be the case–"

"– and that she isn't yet potty trained–"

"– which you also knew – unless she was still talking about Miss P?"

I laughed. "No – as far as I'm aware that is not an issue for Miss P." I reverted to thinking about my daughter. "Anyway, we know it's not unusual for a three-year-old not to be fully potty trained, so why the deep concern?"

Gwyn shrugged her shoulders. "I don't know."

The frustration was almost out of my system now. I'd been summoned to this additional meeting rather against my will, as I didn't see what the teacher could tell me that I didn't already know. Besides, I'd had a quick chat in passing when I picked Eleanor up the other day, so I knew Miss M had the same concerns we did. With all the other events going on in my life it hadn't seemed the most important meeting to attend.

Still, I dutifully turned up that afternoon.

All I could think was *She's not even three! There is so much time for development! Let her enjoy her childhood while she can, enjoy playing, enjoy making friends and running around in the sun. The formal education will come with time.*

But mine was the lone voice fighting the competitive tutoring of international schools. Perhaps their status was judged by getting every child to spell phonetically before they were five? Perhaps they expected her to be the same as Matthew? Perhaps…

"Hello Mummy!"

A fast-moving ball of wet skin and swimsuit flew across the room and gave me a massive hug. "Hi Eleanor!" I planted a big kiss on her cheek, grabbed the towel and pulled her onto my knee.

"Hi Mum!" said Matthew laconically.

"Hi!" I said as he sauntered past. And before Gwyn had a chance to speak Matthew had gone down the corridor to his bedroom.

"Well," Gwyn said, "I know when I'm wanted!"

"You're wanted by me," said Gareth, sauntering in after the kids and planting a big kiss on Gwyn's lips.

"Eurgh!" I said, adding primly, "That's enough of that, thank you! Come, Eleanor, let me take you away from such a to-do."

I finished my gin and tonic and put my glass down.

Eleanor had a big grin on her face. She looked at me intently and held her hand up to my cheek.

"What have you been doing today?" I asked as I carried her to her room.

"'wimmin'," she said, shaking her blonde curls so my face had a short shower.

"Was it fun?"

She nodded her head enthusiastically.

"Who went swimming with you? Did Matthew?"

More nodding.

"Did Emmanuel?" Precious' son often joined them in the pool. Eleanor nodded her assent to that too.

I ceased my questioning, as I knew the answers anyway. I found Precious running a bath and she was immediately of more interest to Eleanor than me. Matthew had already stripped off and Eleanor wriggled until I put her down. I returned to the love-birds, contentedly chatting together on the sofa, to find a refilled glass. *Really, these two ought to get married* I thought.

"Do you want to stay for dinner?" I asked.

"No, I ought to get some marking done," Gwyn said, reluctantly pulling herself up from the sofa. Gareth followed suit.

"That wasn't a request for you to leave," I protested.

Gwyn laughed. "I know, but there's a lot to do and if I don't get a move on I'll never finish."

"I'll walk you home," Gareth said gallantly.

I thought back to that first evening, when Gareth had come round with a chair and her marking had been abandoned for the evening. It was so lovely to see them both together and at ease with each other's lives.

Later it became clear that Gareth was grateful for Gwyn's school workload, as he took the opportunity that evening to ring and ask for my parents-in-law's phone number. He was taking Gwyn away for the weekend and… well, he wanted to speak to her father first, but...

Putting the phone down I was sorry that their engagement was yet another event that Stephen would miss by attending his European conferences. Then I remembered it would be a good occasion to open the bottle of champagne that had been festering in the pantry. I dusted it down and put it in the fridge to chill. Even without Stephen around, I was going to celebrate.

LONDON CALLING

"Right, kids, out we get!"

I climbed out of the car ready to extract the children from their car seats. We'd had our usual Wednesday afternoon at 'babygroup' (mainly toddlers) where the children ran around madly, playing games with their friends. I had sat with the other mothers in the shade, rehydrating with ice-cold drinks. As always, there had been plenty of delicious nibbles and, as I unclipped their seatbelts, I wondered whether we would need to eat anything for tea. I'd have been quite grateful if not, as it was already 5.30 p.m. and the sun was waving goodbye. I had the PTA AGM to attend shortly and I didn't fancy the hassle of cooking.

Just as I had unstrapped Eleanor from her car seat I heard the phone begin to ring. Cursing quietly I grabbed the house keys, unlocked the back door and ran in to catch it before whoever it was rang off. I counted the rings… four… five… six… and snatched the receiver. I was out of breath and completely off guard.

"Hello! Catharine speaking."

There was a pause and then a very polite English voice greeted me from the other end. "Hello. I'm Victoria, a work colleague of Stephen's at the Institute of Child Health."

"Oh, hello." I caught my breath and hissed a stern "Sshh!" at my children as they hurtled past with arms and legs flailing, voices at full throttle. I wondered if Victoria was visiting Zambia and wanted to be in touch with Stephen. I was preparing my 'He's working in the UK' speech then recalled the initial pause on the line: she must have been calling from London.

From London?

That's expensive.

Why is she calling me?

My blood rushed to my feet as a lead weight. I knew this was not a good call.

"Now I don't want you to worry but I have to let you know that Stephen's in hospital."

I was listening and not listening all at once. I knew I had to pay attention, that I had to know exactly what had happened and how to be in touch with him, but all I could think was: *hospital?*

With all the professional detachment yet warmth that medical training offers, Victoria went on to explain what had happened during the day. There was no great emotion, although I could hear the concern in her voice. I'd sent Stephen a brief email in the morning to ask when he'd be calling and whether he'd sorted out some paperwork and had received a peculiar reply at lunchtime which simply said 'I am'. All of a sudden that peculiarity made a modicum of sense. I'd assumed he'd hit 'send' too early, and then had been distracted by other things. Now it appeared this was a sign of him not being well. At all.

Fifteen minutes later, I replaced the handset. The children were running around, shouting at each other. It was dusk. I needed to spray them with mosquito repellent. I had a PTA meeting in an hour. We needed to eat. *My husband's in hospital and can't talk.* I broke down and cried.

"Mummy?"

"Oh, Matthew! Come and give Mum a hug."

He rushed over, his face suffused with confusion over my tears. His little sister toddled after him and I was swept up by their rush of love, blessed by my wonderful children. This made me cry all the more, but it also put things into perspective. *What should I tell them?* I was still processing the information myself. I needed a bit of space before I could let them know their dad was in hospital.

But I had to talk to someone. *Gwyn. Obvious, really. I need to speak to Gwyn.*

The thought of calling her made the tears fall again and there's nothing worse than someone crying at the other end of the phone. I decided to go round.

Matthew reached up to wipe my face. "Why are you crying, Mummy?" he asked.

"Oh, my love, I've just heard some bad news. I'll tell you later, I promise, but just now I must go and see Aunty Gwyn. Shall we see if Precious is free? Maybe she can play your new game with you?"

"Yey!" he cried with a toddler fist pump. "Let's go!"

All concern for my well-being gone in the refreshing way children have, he practically dragged me out of the house and down the path towards Precious' house. I met her halfway: just seeing her made me cry again, tears I tried to hold back as I spoke.

"What's wrong?" she asked, gently touching my arm.

Tearfully I explained I needed to talk to Gwyn and asked if she could look after the children. "Stephen's not well," I said, which was as close to the truth as I could voice.

"Of course," she said with a gentle smile, and whisked the children away to make tea. It would be beans on toast, but I was neither bothered nor interested. I left the house, craving personal space, and headed across the road to see Gwyn.

It was only a three-minute walk through the school grounds but my mind was racing. *What do I tell her?*

She was surprised to see me, apparently early for the PTA meeting in the building next door. It took supreme acting on my part as I welcomed a cup of tea and sat down to chat. Somehow I told her that Victoria had rung, and slowly explained what she'd said.

Stephen had been at his usual desk all morning and had gone for a meeting at the London School of Hygiene and Tropical Medicine. On his return he hadn't seemed right, hadn't been talking properly and the notes he was scribbling weren't making any sense, so Victoria had decided to go with him to his routine diabetic appointment at St Thomas' Hospital. They'd tested his blood sugar levels and found them normal, although he was acting as if he was hypoglycaemic, so they decided to hospitalise him. They didn't know what was wrong.

"He's still not talking properly," I said. "It's like he's had a stroke and he can't find the words to use, so comes out with mumbo jumbo. Or nothing at all."

Gwyn was staring at me, full of compassion, and came over with a box of tissues to give me a hug as I broke down again.

"Oh, I'm sorry," I said, wiping my eyes.

"That's OK. He's my brother, don't forget." And then I realised why she was the best person to talk to.

She knew him and understood both him and his history of diabetes. Indeed, as I thought about it, she'd lived through the days of his diagnosis and initial care: she probably knew far more about it than I did.

And she cared for him as much as I did.

Then it dawned on me I would have to tell her parents, a job I didn't want to undertake.

Gwyn was an absolute rock. Being a teacher at the school she was obliged to go to the AGM but offered me her house to stay in if I wanted. I considered it, then thought that actually doing something with others was better than being alone with my thoughts.

I sat in a little haze of my own, listening to all that the PTA had done over the past year and what they had spent their money on. As usual, the attendance consisted of all the teaching staff, the existing committee and a handful of others. It was barely enough to remain viable and I dreaded the moment they asked for new blood. I shrank into my seat, praying for invisibility. Another day I might have volunteered: that evening I was not sure if I could even speak without bursting into tears. Our friend Peter had joined us and I was grateful that he volunteered as it took the pressure off me. Gwyn sat between us, stoically supporting me with smiles and hand squeezes that no-one else could see.

It was a long hour that was too soon over. Being near the door, I exited quickly and distanced myself away from the others, including Peter. Gwyn joined me shortly afterwards and told me that she'd told Peter. I was grateful, as I knew that meant he would contact people in the church and they would be praying. All I had to do now was tell my parents-in-law.

"Will you be OK?" she asked.

"Yes." I smiled. "Thank you."

I didn't think to ask if she'd be all right, just said

goodnight and left. On arriving home, my children were fast asleep. I let Precious go before I picked up the phone.

Now I was on my own. The room resounded with the sound of nothing: the sort of silence that is physically pressing in on you, immobilising you, squeezing till you cry in pain. First, I tried calling the hospital but couldn't get through on the number I'd been given. Reluctantly I realised I would have to call Grannie and Grampa without any up-to-date knowledge. Taking a deep breath I made the call. I was thankful that Grampa answered, as he took the information in a matter of fact way. I told him I'd tried to get in touch with the ward but failed and he said he'd let me know if he could.

Another phone call over; only one left to go: to tell my boss I wouldn't be at work in the morning. I wandered around the house doing things of no value other than to make me tired and take my mind off the events of the day, before collapsing into bed and crying myself to sleep.

☙

The alarm blared out news from the World Service waking me from deep sleep. For a brief moment, all was right with the world. Then my sleepiness was jolted into wakefulness as I remembered the events of the previous night.

Daylight didn't make them easier to grasp.

What if my husband can never speak again?

What if, from now on, he is a vegetable?

What if I have to spend my life looking after him, translating his mumbles for others?

And then my thoughts flitted to more practical issues. *What if he can't work anymore?*

What will we live on?
Will I have to go back to work full-time?
Will we have to return to London?

I was barely five minutes into the day and had already buried myself under a list of 'what ifs'. They were the same 'what ifs' as the night before, and nothing had changed.

I sat up and shook my head, trying to free my brain of such thoughts. It was a new day. I had no obligation to be at work until Monday. Until I spoke with Stephen, or the hospital, I wouldn't know what the prognosis was. I was desperate to speak with him. However, though it was 6 a.m. in Zambia (daylight, and time to get up, as school started at 7.25 a.m.) the UK was an hour behind and probably wouldn't appreciate such an early call. First and foremost, my children had to go to school, then I would spend the morning trying to contact the hospital in London. I really wanted to speak to my husband.

Getting up, dressed and having a fairly normal routine helped steady my rocky boat. The children behaved in their usual way, typically boisterous with resultant tardiness. I cajoled them into getting appropriately attired for school and before I knew it we were walking across the road to their respective classes.

Returning, I realised that, once again, I was on my own. This morning I had no Gwyn to support me: she was teaching. I was alone with my thoughts and fears; and the hope of connecting to my husband six thousand miles away via my international telephone line.

At long last I was able to get in touch with the ward. The nurse kindly told me he was as well as could be expected and that he had slept well. She uttered other comforting phrases and told me he had a bedside telephone number that I could call. Five minutes later I was talking directly to Stephen.

"Hello," I said. "How are you?"

"I'm." There was nothing more.

"Don't worry," I said into the silence. "You don't have to talk."

I paused, and could hear the gentle grunts and groans of someone trying to speak but unable to formulate words. "Sshh, don't try to talk. Just listen. I'll talk." *That's all very well*, I thought, *but what was I going to talk about?* "The children are doing fine. They went off to school this morning quite happily. Eleanor has ruined another set of clothes with purple paint. Matthew seems to thrive on Miss Gloria's classroom regime but complains about all the colouring in. Gwyn is going to get me some books so he can begin to learn to read."

"Gd."

More silence. *What else could I say?* "I've told Gwyn. She sends her love. And I've told your mum and dad. I'm sure they'll try to get in touch."

"Hmm."

"Don't worry about anything. We're all fine. I'm looking into coming home to visit you."

"No!" His most coherent word so far.

"Look, I want to be there for you. I'll wait and see what the doctors say later, or how you are tomorrow. Please, don't get upset."

"I—"

It was a tortuous phone call. I was gripping the receiver as if my life depended on it, the hot, sweaty plastic held tightly against my ear as if that would bring him closer.

"I love you," I said. "Don't worry. Everything will be all right."

But as I put the phone down I wondered if that could possibly be true.

❧

I know many people don't believe in God and even more don't go to church, but at times of crisis I wonder how they cope.

My church family were fantastic. Despite my fears, I wasn't left on my own that morning. Margriet and Jenny came over and we drank endless cups of tea. Sherry gave me a great big hug when she arrived for work and baked biscuits, which I enjoyed consuming without calorific guilt. Then, when she'd finished teaching, Gwyn came over for the afternoon, and my mind refocused on the children as we did the usual games and trampolining that amused us so. Well, kept them amused anyway. Gareth arrived after work and took them swimming, giving me a little time to call the hospital for an update.

I kept my routine as normal as possible, while finding out what was happening in London. During the next couple of days Stephen's speech improved and he could say simple two- or three-word sentences coherently, but there was major word loss and an inability to retrieve the right vocabulary. Furthermore, the effort exhausted him and over the telephone it sounded awful. Eventually I decided the best thing was to go back and see him, so I booked tickets on an overnight flight from Johannesburg on Sunday evening.

At church in the morning I knew everyone would be asking me how Stephen was, so I plucked up the courage to stand at the front and tell everyone what had happened rather than repeat myself endlessly in conversation afterwards. I wasn't sure I wanted to stay long enough to chat anyway.

As I explained, as simply as I could, that Stephen was in hospital in London, unable to speak or retrieve words, following some trauma to his brain, I began crying. "I'm sorry," I said. "I promised myself I wouldn't do that." I took a deep breath. The tears were unexpected: I really felt quite calm. "Anyway," I concluded, "I know that at times like these we often feel quite useless, desperate to do something to help but don't know what. So I've come up with a list of things that will really help me."

I listed my needs, ranging from the simple (*I'd really appreciate a lift to the airport this afternoon*), the bizarre (*could someone help by looking after the fish?*) to the downright intrusively presumptive (*I have friends visiting next week: would anyone be prepared to look after them?* I was trusting that a twelve year gap, and the presence of his sister, had mellowed The Irish One: I didn't mention the potato boiling fetish, or the bath down Arthur's seat, or his liability with cars.)

And then the ladies came forward and prayed with and for me. One prayed for travelling mercies, particularly crossing London, which I hadn't even begun to think about. At the end of the service I was overwhelmed by offers of help.

❧

Fifteen hours of travel and my children were superb. The flight attendants on the hop down to Johannesburg provided them with an activity bag, as did the ones on the long-haul flight to Heathrow. Together we wandered around Jo'burg airport, the children sitting nicely for a drink and a muffin before the flight. By the time the plane left it was nearly 11 p.m. and they hadn't been crotchety at all. This late departure also meant that they weren't reluctant to fall asleep. We arrived in London surprisingly refreshed.

The prayer for travelling mercies came into my head

as I made my way to the hospital. It may have been only two years since we had lived in London but my fuddled brain was uncertain what type of ticket to purchase for the Underground. I had chosen the Heathrow Express into Paddington and then couldn't remember how to get to Westminster. I told my children to wait with the suitcases, while I walked over to look at the map next to the ticket machines.

A Tube official kindly reprimanded me. He didn't think I should leave my young children alone, even for the three metres I had walked. I looked back at my bronzed children, smaller than the cases they guarded, brightly dressed in comparison to the drab, grey commuters. He was probably right, but what choice did I have? The place was busy on a Monday morning and I presumed it would be less trouble to everyone if I left them standing aside from the queue.

"Children get lost," he told me. I read into this: abducted. Then I remembered the travelling mercies and trusted God.

Together the three of us plodded through the underground system, traipsing along brightly-lit corridors to the platforms, standing well back and then methodically getting onto the train. My boy wasn't yet five, but I charged him with all sorts of responsibilities.

"If the train leaves with you on but not me, get off at the next station and wait. I'll be on the next train. And stay together, whatever happens."

He nodded solemnly at me, but the excitement of trains and travel was great. Thankfully it all went without a hitch. At Westminster the advent of the Jubilee line meant that there were easy lifts for us to catch together and soon we were marching over Westminster Bridge towards the imposing tower that is St Thomas' Hospital. Not a single whimper did I hear.

It was a brisk, sunny, autumnal day and being out in

the fresh air was good for us all. Matthew and Eleanor held hands, their little rolling suitcases containing their personal belongings trundling beside them. Here the pavement was wide enough for us to walk abreast, and I watched their determination with pride. No more need of prams and pushchairs: I had two independent world-travellers, though I had the two large suitcases. As I crossed the bridge I was quite calm and collected. By the time I passed the Lupus building and was about to enter the Main Entrance I was terrified. What was I going to find?

THE BRAIN EVENT

Stop.

The world stopped. Nothing else mattered. My parents-in-law were looking after the children a hundred miles away and I barely thought about them. My life had shrunk to a one metre radius around a hospital bed: to the man I loved.

There was nothing for me to do but sit and wait. We didn't talk much. He couldn't properly communicate: a few words or a jumbled sentence exhausted him. Mostly he just slept, and I watched, hoped, worried.

When will this get better?

What future is there – for us, for him, for our family?

How will we survive if my doctor husband can't doctor any more?

Can I cope? I'm not the most patient of people. Can I possibly look after an invalid for the rest of his life?

I love his mind: his wit, his intelligence, his thoughts. What if they never come back?

He slept on, unaware of my trauma while coping with his own.

When he woke I held his hand, offered him water, waited. He tried to talk, but stumbled and faltered. He couldn't find words – simple words, that we both knew he knew, but which were lost inside a brain with broken connections.

One afternoon he had to complete a test where he merely had to name the pictures he was shown. Cat. Dog. Ball. Piano. Computer. Lawnmower. His frustration was immense when he couldn't remember a word. How does the brain know it knows, yet still be unable to retrieve the knowledge?

Later he asked me what the machine was that goes tick-tick-tick, regularly. "For music," he added.

"A metronome?"

"That's it," he spat out. "A metronome," he repeated to himself, re-learning a vocabulary he had lost. "A metronome."

I thought he was being hard on himself, as it wasn't a word everyone would be expected to know and locate, even in full health.

But the talking tired him out. I told him not to talk. Just listen.

I filled him in on what news I had.

I told him about Matthew's first day at school: about how proud I was of him, my grown-up little boy. About how he squirmed in front of the camera as I took a photo of him before we left. How he squinted into the sun. How he held my hand tightly as we walked across the road to the school, and then stood in line, glad to see some of his old friends from pre-school after a long summer holiday.

And then how he was away – gone, without a

backward glance. My baby boy in 'big school'.

How it had been a much longer walk home for me, alone.

He smiled. I knew he'd heard.

☙

Another day of waiting. I listened as the doctors came round. There was the official ward round, once a day, then a string of specialists who wanted to understand what had happened. He was principally under the care of the diabetic consultant, but the neurologists were keen to have an understanding too.

The chief consultant appeared with a train of eager students behind him, breezily asking if it was OK for them to ask him questions.

"Of course," the patient-doctor mumbled in reply.

A student asked some standard questions, such as what medicine he was on and whether he had taken it correctly. The patient-doctor replied with precision (to the milligram) and the student had the perfect case history.

The consultant asked the student what she noticed about the patient.

"The answers are perfect," she responded.

"And what does that make you think?" the consultant led her on.

A pause. "He's probably a medic?"

The consultant smiled. "Precisely."

But he didn't have any answers. No answers to the real questions. *Why is my husband like this? What happened? When will he be back to normal?* Or, the most worrying question: *will he ever be normal again?*

The consultant drew the curtains with the flair that comes of routine and swooshed away down the corridor.

❧

Stephen didn't have any other visitors as all our family were far away and I hadn't told many people what had happened. One afternoon, though, our church minister, a friend, came to visit. He chatted gently, softly, comfortingly, though the conversation was hugely one-sided. He prayed. He spoke words of support and reassurance, and left.

The exhausted patient slept. It was all too much.

I wanted to weep.

❧

I had to leave. I'd exceeded all visiting hours, probably only excused because I had travelled such a distance. I had no home in London, just lodging with friends. Still, I decided that Stephen should rest and I should probably buy a gift for my temporary landlords. I also thought I should call in at the Institute and talk with Victoria, the doctor who had made that fateful call to me in Zambia. She, too, deserved a thank you present.

Leaving Stephen to sleep I felt quite chirpy as I picked up my bag to go shopping. I had the whole of London at my feet and, though there was a chill in the air, it was a bright autumnal day.

Near the nurses' station I was collared by the consultant.

"Mrs Withenay, could you answer a few questions?"

Though his opening made it sound as if I was about to be interrogated by the police, I acquiesced.

"Have you noticed any changes in your husband recently?"

"No."

"Have his blood sugars been normal?"

"I think so. At least, as normal as they ever are."

"Has he been sleeping OK?"

"Well, yes." My voice faltered. I hadn't seen him for the previous month, so maybe he hadn't been sleeping well. Maybe his blood sugars had been all askew. How was I to know?

"Did you have any inkling that there could be something wrong?"

No! I want to scream. *No! No! No! Don't you think I'd have done something about it if I had?*

"No. Not a clue," I said quietly, shaking my head and looking at the floor. He was wearing brogues. I wondered how he didn't slip on the polished hospital floor.

Lifting my head, I could see confusion written across his face. It didn't add up. There was no logical explanation for what had happened.

"Well, thank you Mrs Withenay," he said, graciously. Thus dismissed, I left for my shopping trip.

As I stepped into the lift, my loneliness took hold and my mind went into overdrive.

I should have known.

I should have seen the signs. Of what, I'm not sure. No-one seems sure.

But it is my fault: I should have seen it coming.

I should take more notice; care more; worry less about the children and more about him.

The joy of being free to shop in the big city lost its charm and I quietly sat in the hospital canteen with a mug of tea and the largest, most chocolatey muffin I could find.

෴

The next day there was a new test for Stephen to undergo.

We were taken to a quiet room the other side of the hospital. Stephen lay on the bed, in the centre of the room, with electric nodes stuck to his head; wires strung out like a barmy hairdo. I sat silently behind the specialist and peered over her shoulder. The computer monitor recorded wavelengths: wiggly lines across a blank page. A comforting blip-blip-blip sounded as time ticked by

Occasionally the specialist asked him a question and the lines would jump about, shaken by the need to process information and regurgitate an answer. But mostly it was quiet, calming. The lighting was not bright and the interrogation was not complicated.

After a period of silence I noticed the lines grew flatter, almost petering out. I wondered if he was dying on the bed in front of me, but a gentle word from the doctor and he opened his eyes. The soporific atmosphere had allowed him to drift into sleep.

Awake again, we returned to the ward for lunch. Stephen spooned hospital food slowly into his mouth, time taken as much due to its non-appetising appearance as to his difficulty to fully coordinate movement. I had yet another pre-packaged sandwich from the shop on the ground floor. I was working my way through their range, perked up by the occasional packet of crisps.

We chatted, hopeful that the morning's test would explain what had happened, what damage might have been incurred and the prospects for recovery.

Between mouthfuls I told him a little more about Gwyn and Gareth's engagement. I loved that Gareth had asked discreetly for Stephen's parents' phone number, so he could pop the question in the traditional fashion. He'd then taken Gwyn away for the weekend, to South Luangwa, to one of the most beautiful places on earth.

"They came back and told Mike and Rache first, of course," I said, "and by the time they got to our house it was a little too late to start on the champagne I'd got for them, but Gwyn was grinning from ear to ear, the happiest girl in Christendom."

Stephen had finished his food and lay back on the pillows, drained and exhausted by the morning's activities.

"Their plan is for a wedding in the spring," I rabbited on, then faltered and fell quiet. Stephen was asleep.

I looked at him in peaceful repose and wondered: *will he be able to make it?*

What sort of a wedding will it be for Gwyn if her brother is unable to speak, or unwilling to be out in public?

Could we possibly celebrate alongside this?

I could have wasted my life wondering 'what if'. There was no solution but patience. When the report on the morning's brain test eventually came back at the end of the day it was succinct and factual.

"There is damage… delay… difficulty…."

But the specialist didn't have any answers.

～

It had been over a week since I'd arrived and Stephen was making steady progress. Physically he was nearly functioning as normal, although everything exhausted him and coherent sentences were only just joining up into paragraph lengths. I spent most of my time sitting beside his bed, reading and waiting, or talking with him if he was up for it.

However, this particular morning Stephen had disappeared – to the toilet, down the corridor, anywhere but here. In contrast, I was nosey. I wanted to see what happened and how the system worked. "City

Hospital" was being filmed, and that day would include a focus on this particular ward. I stayed in my usual chair, reading the newspaper, trying not to chew the end of the pen.

Everyone on the ward was preened, sitting upright in bed, their pyjamas straightened and hair brushed. I don't know if the Queen's arrival would have had more fuss made, but the prospect of being on television spruced everyone up.

In came the presenter, Ainsley Harriott, with a TV producer and a consultant. They chatted with the yellow man in the next-door bed, running through the questions Ainsley was going to ask, then listening to the reply. At the appointed time, when the show was live on TV, they returned together with the cameraman and sound technician. The same questions were asked, more efficiently answered, and then the camera stopped rolling.

Ainsley spoke kindly to the man, and then cheerfully to the rest of us in the bay of the ward, smiling, encouraging.

It was my moment of television fame as the camera panned past me.

Stephen returned from hiding and I gleefully told him what had happened. Now I knew he was getting better, as he was not so ill that he could not perceive an embarrassment in being seen in a hospital bed.

"I can't be seen like that," he said later. "What would people think? They'd never respect my work again."

I held back from shouting a retort. It was a daytime TV programme and I didn't think the prime audience was likely to be other doctors or researchers, nor that the viewers would pay much attention to him as a patient in the background.

Instead I told him not to worry. "Anyone worth listening to will respect you for who you are, and your work for its results, regardless of a spell in hospital," I said, then changed the conversation to focus on the concise crossword in the newspaper. We'd realised that this was an excellent way for him to rebuild his vocabulary, to reconnect the meanings and subtle inferences of the English language.

"Before we do today's, shall we see what yesterday's answers were?"

⁂

It was Friday and Stephen had now been in hospital for over two weeks. At long last, he was frustrated.

"When are they coming?" he said irritably.

"They'll be here soon. They haven't forgotten you," I said, pacifying him by walking to the end of the bay to see if I could see the doctors on their ward round.

"I just want to get out of here," he said. "I'm taking up a bed that someone else could use."

It was a sure sign that he was functioning as normal again.

"Don't get your hopes up too much," I cautioned. "Wait and see what the consultant says. They're the experts, you know."

"Yes, yes…" he replied, drumming his fingers on the bedsheets as he waited.

Eventually we were treated to a visit by two neurological consultants.

"Well?"

"We can see from your scans that it wasn't a stroke. There is no evidence of permanent damage," said one.

"It might have been a viral infection," said the other.

"Or it might have been a hypoglycaemic attack," said the first.

There was a pause.

"We don't know what happened," they admitted.

"All we can do is call it 'a brain event'."

A brain event? My husband had been in a first-world, top international hospital with some of the best neurological consultants on the globe, for two weeks. He'd had endless tests and scans and assessments, and the considered medical opinion was: *he's had a brain event.*

I wasn't sure what to say.

"Can he leave?"

"Yes. Go home and rest, and come back for a check-up in six weeks."

Six weeks? What would we do for six weeks? Where would we stay?

"Can he fly?"

There was a hesitation as the consultants glanced at one another.

"It's a risk," one of them said. "Not knowing what has happened, the changes in air pressure could set off another incident."

"But that's where home is," I pleaded. "Is it possible?"

Reluctantly, cautiously, they agreed to let him fly.

He could go home.

I could take him home.

The waiting was over: *what now?*

ROUTINE RESUMES

Along our street, high overhead, the jacarandas were waving in the breeze, delicate mauve flowers saying 'good day' to the sun and complementing the clear blue sky. The potholed, dusty orange road was bordered by their fallen petals, as the season moved towards the hottest part of the year. At the end of the road were some flamboyants, their vibrant green leaves contrasting with their emerging red flowers. The avenue of colour welcomed us home.

In our absence another ceiling panel had fallen in, spraying the kitchen with a mixture of dirt and termites. The landlord was very efficient sending his two men round to fix the problem, but I could see that it was going to ripple along the length of the room. I asked the men what they were going to do about the termites in the roof.

"We will spray," one of them said.

"What with? And where?"

"The roof," he said, pointing at the roof space above. "Anti-termite spray."

He was getting out his spray gun when I stopped him. No consideration had been given to the spraying of chemicals into an open void above my kitchen, where we prepared all the food. I didn't know exactly what was in his concoction but I was certain I didn't want to consume it. In the end I decided that a gradual collapse of ceiling panels was preferable to the wholesale fumigation of the house.

As the October heat took hold our garden browned and we, like everyone else, slowed down. My routine resumed: a mix of part-time work hours and running the house. I still met up with friends, but for the most part the intensity of a conversation with others was too much for Stephen. He didn't return to work immediately: even a day spent at home exhausted him. His sleep patterns were disrupted and his blood sugar levels were almost impossible to control. We eliminated the obvious (insulin too cold at the back of the fridge, insulin too warm having been kept out of the fridge too long) and were left with the realisation that it was going to be a long haul back to health.

Stephen's conscience took over after a couple of weeks, though, and he began to ease himself back into work. He could only work a half day before coming home to sleep, and required the next day off to recover from the exertion. I tried not to get frustrated – either with his exhaustion, his lack of language skills or his determination to work despite the extent of his illness. The protestant work ethic had a powerful hold over his conscience: the research, the malnourished children and the testing of samples consumed his energy.

"The problem is that when he's home he's asleep!" I

moaned to Margriet and Jenny.

Our Friday meet-up at the café kept me sane. In the weeks since The Brain Event these women had simply been there. I'd been able to retreat inside myself while listening to the goings-on of their families and it had been the most therapeutic experience. Of course, they were concerned about me and (more so) about Stephen, but there was no interrogation, just space.

On this occasion, though, I was venting my anger. "Honestly! It's so selfish! He goes to the hospital, giving the best of his day to his work and then comes home to sleep. The children's sole interaction with him yesterday was to complain about his snoring!"

"Ach, but it's better than the alternative," said Margriet.

My shoulders sagged. "I know," I said, recalling the man I had found in a hospital bed a month earlier.

"Is he in touch with the consultants in the UK? Have they any explanations?"

I shook my head. "He's flying back at the end of next week for ten days so they can check him over, but they seem pleased with his progress. Still no explanation as to what happened, or why, or how, but at least he is improving. His speech is functional, if simple. The doctors say he'll just need to keep taking things slowly."

"That won't please him!"

"No – not much! Then again, he gets so tired and worn out that he doesn't have much choice."

"Is he still doing the crosswords?" asked Jenny.

"Yes. I think he's getting better at them, but they drain him. Who would have thought he'd be so exhausted by a book of concise crosswords!"

The lingering symptoms of The Brain Event were a loss of words, or word associations. It had become apparent before we had left the UK that he needed exercises to re-establish the links, treating him as if he were a stroke patient. The book of Times Crosswords I'd bought from the WRVS at St Thomas' hospital before we left was his daily exercise. The answers were dependent on a thesaurus-like linking of the words and meanings rather than the cryptic play on letters and anagrams. He'd still not completed a whole one all by himself.

"What I find hardest," I explained, "is that I'm often dying to answer the questions for him. Some of the clues are so obvious, and yet he cannot find the words. It can be so frustrating – more so for him as he knows he ought to know the answer, and can tell that I know it, but he simply cannot locate it."

"He didn't seem to have any problems last week when we were chatting," said Margriet. She was right: he could manage short conversations, short interactions with others, and no-one would suspect anything was wrong. Basic language skills were there, and he'd recovered enough to be able to find some words, even though there were better, more accurate ones available.

"No, it's easier with friends. You have some understanding and a lot of patience. It's a bit similar to Eleanor, struggling to find words and making herself understood." In so many ways I now had two three-year-olds developing their language skills in the house. At least there was nothing but time holding either of them back, though I didn't always have the patience to allow time to do its work.

"Any news on the funding?" Jenny asked.

"Not yet: I think he's expecting a phone call about that this afternoon. His supervisors are confident he'll get it, but there's a lot of rigmarole and hoop-jumping to go through first."

"What are you hoping for?"

"He's applying to have a further six months, based on having had a month off sick, another month pretty much off sick, and anticipating the next few months being on and off. We're taking it easy up to Christmas at the very least."

"That sounds wise," said Jenny. "You can see how things are after that."

"The main problem remains the diabetes," I said. "Somehow he just can't get it fully under control."

Whatever he did, the hypos and hypers kept coming around; highs and lows of blood sugar concentration in the blood. Neither extreme was very good. When hyper he felt ill, with a desperate headache and nausea. When hypo anything could happen. It was possible to fall into a coma from being hypo, but normally he went white as a sheet and started acting peculiarly.

"Worst case scenario, he'll have to check his bloods every four hours, even through the night, and take insulin or sugar accordingly. I wouldn't mind, but I know that means *me* being woken by an alarm in the middle of the night and him sleeping through it."

"I can well imagine!"

"Pumps have just been made available," I continued. "They're permanently attached and constantly drip insulin into your blood stream. It means you can control your blood sugar levels at the press of a button."

"That sounds perfect!" said Jenny.

"Far fewer injections, and you get to sleep through the night," said Margriet astutely.

"Unsurprisingly that is quite appealing! But the doctors are unwilling to trial Stephen on one while we're living here. As soon as he goes back to living in the UK he'll be able to apply for one. Just not right now."

"Do you think you should move back?"

There was an awkward silence. I'd never considered doing that – not once. Not even at the worst point, when I was unsure whether he'd be able to walk and talk again, when I thought I might be married to a vegetable for life. I'd never considered moving back to the UK. From my perspective I was just carrying on as planned.

But maybe that was what we should do. Maybe we should put Stephen's health before his research, in advance of his career. The doctors weren't happy with the thought of us returning to Zambia after he was hospitalised two months earlier. He'd survived the long haul flight: was that enough to declare him well?

"We're seeing how things go up to Christmas," I said. "After that... who knows?"

It was the best answer I could give.

CALLED INTO SCHOOL – AGAIN

We had been called into school. Something was wrong.

"We would like to have a chat with you about Eleanor."

Oh, teachers. You phrase it so gently, almost innocuously. What can be scary about a chat?

"It is probably best if you both come. Would Wednesday be OK?"

Both of us? This meant Stephen had to have an awake day: take time away from work. The chat became terrifying.

But I dismissed it. It had to be because Eleanor, at three years old, didn't talk properly. She had some words – clear, distinct words – and could always get her own way, but fluent sentences were yet to materialise. *But Matthew didn't talk until three. She's happy and can get what she wants, so why worry?*

But I was worried. It was the second time I'd been called in by a teacher to discuss Eleanor that term.

The meeting was awful. Five fully-grown adults crouched on toddler chairs around a low table. Bright chirpy parents; serious, concerned teachers.

"Eleanor is a lovely girl, but…"

Never a good way to start.

"We are concerned that she is not participating fully in class. As soon as she moved up into Red group it was noticed that she wasn't behaving normally."

They tried to speak so gently, to soften the blow, but we were shocked. Our beautiful, bright girl was struggling. Really struggling. Not just not talking, but her behaviour was abnormal for a child her age. It had been nearly a full term. *Why didn't they tell us sooner?*

"We wanted to be sure, so the head of department has been in to observe as well. And we delayed meeting until today so that the school psychologist could see her too."

Psychologist? What is wrong with my girl?

"She is very quiet. She doesn't seem to be paying any attention to instructions. When asked to go and sit on the mat, she will walk off to the play area."

MY GIRL IS NORMAL! I wanted to shout.

"We wondered what she was like at home. Does she follow instructions?"

She was a normal, obstreperous, three-year-old girl. Sometimes she did, sometimes she didn't.

"How does she interact with, say, Matthew, or other children?"

They were siblings: they fought and cared for each other in equal measure. She'd play quietly by herself, or games with Sherry, or run boisterously around the garden.

"We've noticed that she doesn't socialise with the other children. At playtime, she plays by herself in the sandpit. She barely talks."

It was a punch in the stomach.

I didn't care if Eleanor couldn't speak properly yet, or if she couldn't hop (something the teachers were concerned about) or if she couldn't spell her name (she was three!) but socialising: that was high on my agenda.

I could have wept. *This is my beautiful daughter. She is happy and cheerful. She loves life, runs around, laughs with joy!*

How did this character change occur?

Why did we not spot it?

I wanted her to be normal, like all the other children. But she was not. She was anything but.

❧

Stephen had to return to work after the meeting while I was left alone in the house. I wandered aimlessly around in the kitchen, listening to Sherry and Matthew playing with Eleanor. There were giggles and laughs. I heard Sherry counting their jumps on the trampoline.

"… eighteen, nineteen, twenty. OK! Eleanor's turn."

I made another cup of tea. *It might help.* Certainly it gave me something to do, even if only for a couple of minutes.

What has happened? My world, so gradually being pieced together again after The Brain Event, had fallen apart again in the space of a couple of hours. There was too much for me to digest and I yearned for Stephen's company. This was something we should have been facing together, but I was on my own. I knew that his work was important, and that with lab experiments things have to be done at precise times so he had to be there but… Sometimes it would have been nice if they were ignored and I could have had my husband instead.

I sighed. His patients were dying. My daughter was alive and well.

In some respects nothing had changed. The giggles I heard from the garden were the same as yesterday's, and the ones the day before.

Just as we were getting some resemblance of normality back with Stephen, life was turned upside down again. My carefree daughter needed help. She had to be able to play with others and to act appropriately in class. *What if there was something wrong – seriously wrong? What if Eleanor was going to require special needs education for the rest of her life? What if she didn't socialise and we, her parents and family, were the only people she'd talk to? What would her teenage, adult years be like then?*

Tea was made and, having snaffled a couple of choc chip cookies from the tin, I felt a little more able to cope. First things first: she might be deaf.

The psychologist had suggested this and recommended that we had her hearing tested. The teacher was going to place Eleanor near her when sitting in a circle, to ensure that she heard her instructions properly. It was a small but hopefully significant move.

Meanwhile I was faced with the task of finding a hearing test in Zambia: more specifically, a hearing test that I could trust and rely upon. We were members of a reputable medical clinic that had many Western medical facilities. Friends had spoken highly of its ante- and post-natal care, so I expected them to have a lot of services for children. To date, we had barely had to use them: there were advantages to being married to a paediatrician.

I found their number and picked up the phone.

"Good afternoon, madam, how may I help you?"

"I am phoning on behalf of my daughter. The school have noticed behavioural problems that may be due to her hearing. Do you provide hearing tests, and if so, when?"

"Madam, I am sorry, but we do not do hearing tests here."

"What? None at all?"

Bottom fell out of world.

"No, madam. I am sorry."

"Do you know if any of the other clinics do them?"

"No. You have to go to UTH."

"UTH?"

"Yes, UTH. Go to the audiology department and make an appointment there."

"UTH. OK. Thank you." My voice was flat as I put the phone down. UTH. University Teaching Hospital. The last place I wanted to go to get medical care for my children. Stephen had already dismissed their audiology services so, while I was prepared to give it a go, I knew that we would have no faith in their results.

I raided the biscuit tin again. The hips might not like it, but sometimes needs must. It was all I could do to hold back from pouring some alcohol, but I had a mug of tea in hand. Chocolate would work its magic.

I paced around the kitchen. The options before me were to have a hearing test at UTH (wouldn't trust the outcome) or wait until we were back in the UK. Alternatively we could go to South Africa and get a test done privately, but it would cost. Flights, hotels, appointments. *Could I let Stephen take her? Probably not.* All my maternal instincts said I had to be there with her, every step of the way, despite Stephen's medical expertise. I'd carried her those first nine months, I'd given birth to her, I'd postponed my career for her: the marrow in my bones said I must travel with her. *So do I take Matthew as well? Do we all go, doubling the cost?* I'd already blown the emergency flights budget with Stephen's Brain Event.

Insurance! The thought hit me like a bullet. I went through to the office and rummaged around to find the insurance certificate. Pulling out the contract, I read the small print, front to back. It was not a condition that was known about before we took out the insurance, but outpatient costs were not necessarily covered. Costs of travel for assessments in other countries were covered if the tests could not be done in the country of residence. The receptionist had said that UTH could do the tests: I concluded that we would have to pay.

I put down the booklet and looked to the heavens. We could probably have argued our way through this, but it was going to cause nothing but grief.

Filled with despair, I returned to the kitchen. *Stuff his work – I'm going to call Stephen and see if he has any ideas. Perhaps he'll reconsider his opinion of UTH's services?*

"Hi! How are you?"

"Fine. How are you?"

"Fine." I gave a nervous snicker. "We've been here too long. We even greet each other like Zambians."

He laughed. I clung to the phone, loving this man who held our family together and always put a smile on my face.

"Have you any news? How's Eleanor?"

"She's fine, playing outside with Matthew and Sherry. You wouldn't know there was anything wrong." I held my breath. In the silence I knew we were both thinking the worst. "I rang the clinic," I said, and then recounted the conversation I'd had.

"Bother!" he said. I felt he was being extremely restrained.

I waited to hear his thoughts.

"I don't exactly know what services UTH offer. I fear they'll be quite basic. Really, you need someone highly skilled to administer and interpret hearing tests."

"So UTH is a no-go?"

"Well, if it's the only choice then we must investigate it further. I'll see what I can find out, who's in charge and so on. But I guess we should focus on the South African option."

I took a deep breath. "All right. I'll look into the costs and times of flights and stuff like that. When are you likely to be home?"

"I hope to leave in about an hour."

"Good," I said quietly. "See you then."

He'd be home in a couple of hours (I was now more accurate at interpreting his timescales than he was). In the meantime, I could go on-line and find out about the South Africa options and cook dinner. Attacking some vegetables might do wonders for my frustrations.

Twenty minutes later my phone rang. It was Stephen.

"Eckhard," he said without preamble.

"Eckhard?"

"Yes, Eckhard. Phone Eckhard. The charity he works for does hearing tests. Ask him what he thinks of UTH's services."

Eckhard, our dear friend. Of course.

A minute later (possibly less) I was on the phone to him.

"Eckhard, I'm sorry to bother you at work."

"No problem," he said, "no problem at all." Mentally I pictured him waving his arm in the air dismissively. I smiled.

"We have a small problem. We need to have Eleanor's hearing tested. The clinic tells us they're only done at UTH. What is their service like? Would we be better waiting until we get to the UK?"

"Well, I'm sure the UK will be better than UTH. No, UTH services are not good."

I took a deep breath. It was what I expected to hear, but at every stage I held out hope that the news would be better. So far today, everything had gone from bad to worse.

"But," Eckhard continued, "we have a Dutch ENT

surgeon arriving on Saturday for three weeks. He could see Eleanor."

"Really?" I could hardly believe my own ears.

"Sure! I'll speak with him when he arrives and arrange an appointment."

"Oh, Eckhard, that is great! Thank you! Thank you so much."

"No problem!" he said, with his German efficiency, and ended the phone call.

I hopped and skipped around the kitchen. There was hope! There was hope.

THE RETURN OF THE ACTORRATOR

The worst bit was waiting.

What is going on in there? What are they doing to my daughter?

Will she survive the operation?

I had brought a book to read, but couldn't because tears were streaming down my face. I was trusting my child to have a general anaesthetic in an operating room in Lusaka, Zambia. In Africa. Never, never had I thought I would do this.

The last two weeks had gone by in a bit of a blur. Eckhard's contact saw Eleanor the day after he arrived and diagnosed glue ear. Unbeknown to us her ears had filled with gunge and she required grommets to drain them. She had probably been 95% deaf for some time.

The relief of diagnosis had been overtaken by the anxiety about an operation. Little over a week later and I was waiting outside an operating theatre, entrusting Eleanor to a Dutch surgeon. And Margriet, Eckhard's wife. She was a fully trained nurse and had offered to go into the operating theatre with Eleanor. They had been pillars of support over the previous couple of weeks.

I sat on the wooden bench, waiting. The walls were painted blue. Not a cheery blue, but a colour that wouldn't be out of place on a battleship. There was no-one else around. This was not the hustle and bustle of UTH, thronged with people, but was the Lusaka Eye Hospital on the edge of town. I idly wondered why there were not wards full of inpatients.

Friends had reassured me this was a minor operation, a standard procedure. I knew that, but all their examples were from the West, or South Africa. One was from Zimbabwe. Her eldest daughter had had grommets fitted.

"The worst bit was the anaesthetic," she'd said. "I was holding her and then suddenly, she's a dead weight."

Dead. That's what frightened me. Any operation carried risks. General anaesthetics could go wrong, even on the simplest and most routine procedure. Complications could arise. Could this hospital cope with it? Could the Zambian healthcare system deal with an emergency?

Worst of all, I was going through all this on my own. Stephen was back in the UK for his check up with the neurologists. The timing was poor, but there were only so many flights to and from the UK that our budget could accommodate. I was left to look after our daughter through the operation and recovery. Not that I'd been given long to dwell on matters when we arrived, as Eleanor was first on the list (and the only patient I'd seen) and we had been rushed through by the surgeon's wife. To them we were late arrivals, although I like to think we were on time, particularly by African standards.

I heard her crying. I imagined the anaesthetics being administered: she clearly didn't like the needle. I couldn't hold back my tears. *Hold on there, little girl. It'll be OK. Oh, Lord, please look after my baby. Please bring her through.*

A door opened and closed, then Margriet was standing in front of me.

"Do you want to see her? She is out now."

I stumbled to my feet, knocking my basket over in the process. "Finished? Already?"

"Yes."

I stuffed my unread book away and grabbed the basket. "But I just heard her crying," I said, following Margriet back through the double doors.

"That was her coming round. See!"

And there, in the corridor, a small child on a big hospital bed was bawling her eyes out.

"Sshh! Hey, little one! It's Mummy!"

I rushed to her side, bags falling to the floor beneath the trolley.

"Don't cry. It's all over. Mummy's here."

I held her hand and stroked her forehead.

"Sshh! Don't cry."

I was no great role model, as tears poured down my face. Tears of relief, for Eleanor was still alive. Now she had grommets, her hearing would improve and so should her attitude and behaviour at school. Fear had vanished; hope had risen.

I kissed her tears away. "Mummy's here. Always."

❧

It was Friday, school assembly day, and the day that my son took his first steps onto the big school stage.

We had practised all week. His words were typed out and stuck on the back of the gold present. He was reading three sentences and did it brilliantly. At least he did at home, when I stood one end of the corridor and he the other, shouting as loudly and clearly as he could.

But now rehearsals were over and it was time for the show. I ran madly round the house, slurping my mug of tea and grabbing the camera (thank goodness the battery was charged). I cursed myself for being a terrible mother: *why do I always run late?* Slamming down the mug on the side I called to Sherry.

"I'm off!"

"Goodbye, madam," she responded. She was calmly drying the dishes as I fretted and ran around, and I knew that within minutes my mug would have been washed, dried and put away. Her peaceful attitude calmed my mania.

I only lived across the road from the school, but my timing was tight. *Or am I worrying excessively? After all, I will be there in time: I just might not get the best seat.* There were thirty other mothers thinking the same thing about their children. *I want the best view of my son's moment of glory; the fight is on for the front row.*

Watching my eldest child grow up brought back so many memories of my own childhood. I remembered my first school assembly had been a personal disaster. I must have been terrified, for I had had to speak first, open the assembly with a 'Good morning everyone!' but I had clammed up completely and ran to hide behind Miss Chrone, who had gracefully stood in to say my lines instead.

Thank goodness Matthew is a confident young boy and has practised hard.

Arriving at the school, I settled myself into a chair

253

next to some friends in the multi-purpose hall. It wasn't a bad spot: front row, fairly central. We were all early.

The multi-purpose hall wouldn't pass the Trades Descriptions Act, were that to exist in Zambia. It was a vast space that comfortably seated the whole school. There were no walls, just steel pillars set into the concrete base holding up a corrugated metal roof, in which there are about half-a-dozen air vents which twirled noisily in the wind. It was used for assemblies, with a sound system that improved volume but not audibility. It was used for PE, but the open walls enabled balls to fly off into the field beyond. It was used for concerts, but moving a grand piano from the music room indoors wrecked its tuning more often than not. Because of its open nature, everything had to be put out and then away for each event so nothing could be stolen. The noise from the roof vents when it was windy prevented anything else being heard. During the rainy season, the rain hammered on the metal roof, drowning out everything else. In the summer the area heated like an oven, roasting the audience. There were rumours of it being renamed the multi-useless hall.

We heard the bell sound for the end of break. A few minutes later, the reception classes trouped in, meekly sitting on the stage where their teacher directed. Being the Christmas nativity there was an array of sheep and donkeys, tea-towel-adorned shepherds and tinsel-trimmed angels.

There was one microphone in the centre of the stage and Matthew, bedecked in regal cape and crown, was in the middle of the row of children behind it. They were all perfectly behaved. *Are they nervous? Will any of them buckle under the pressure, as I did all those years ago?*

Slowly the rest of the Primary School filed in, the eldest ones at the back, jostling for a seat, pretending to be big and important. I gave a little wave to Gwyn. She had a video recorder and was going to tape what she could of the event. I was sorry Stephen was missing this momentous occasion. Something about being the first makes it the most special – first steps, first words, first day at school – and Stephen seemed to be missing them all. In contrast, Matthew knew his dad was away and didn't seem all that concerned. *Perhaps, aged five, that is normal? If Stephen were here…* but I had to stop thinking like that. Matthew had me and we were all doing our best to let Stephen know what was happening.

A hushed silence fell over the children as the primary head took the roaming mike and stood at the front.

"Welcome, everyone. Today we have a very special occasion when the reception classes are taking our assembly. These are the youngest children in our school and this is a big event for them and their parents. So, boys and girls, I want you to be particularly quiet as you listen to what they say." He looked over and around all the children, encouraging them by his seriousness. There were a few who shuffled awkwardly, dropping their heads; then the teacher resumed.

"They have worked very hard at this all week and I think we are in for a treat. So, without further ado, I hand you over to Reception."

He walked away from the stage and I heard the click as he switched off the microphone. The teachers stepped forward and made all the children stand.

But what was happening? Matthew was walking towards the microphone. His lines were later: I knew that the Three Wise Men were late in the story (possibly even a year late, but that theological argument was unlikely to be acted out that morning).

Yet there he was, standing up to the mike.

"GoodmorningeveryoneWelcometoourassembly."

The words shot out like bullet fire, and seconds later he was back in line, sitting cross-legged on the stage. I gasped. Everyone else sniggered, or tried to control their laughter, and unwittingly they broke my heart. They were laughing at my son. Silently I screamed *He's only five! He did so well!* Better than I did, all those years ago.

But the show was up and running and nothing stopped it now. Mary staggered with her donkey, a plastic doll lay in a basket of hay, angels frightened shepherds and sheep; the story of Jesus' birth was told again. Towards the end, the lines I was expecting from Matthew were delivered. They came out confidently, firmly, slowly. I sensed everyone eating their words, or their laughter at least, as they heard a five-year-old boy read so much and so well. Maternal pride was restored.

The final lines were spoken, the last song was sung, and the assembly was over. Wild, rapturous applause from the proud parents; polite and much more restrained from the primary school pupils. They filed back to their classrooms while we got a chance to congratulate our children.

"Matthew did so well," my friend said as we walked towards the stage. "My daughter could never read all that."

"Really?" I was slightly incredulous, as Matthew could read so easily. Then I remembered my manners. "But she did really well. I could hear every word."

But inside I was glowing. My little boy had stood up and spoken in public. Today the actorrator had graduated to headline star.

"Well done, boyo!" I said as I approached him. I grinned from ear to ear; he smiled and we revelled in a great big hug.

REINDEER FODDER

We had reached the stage of parenthood when Christmas was an absolute joy with the children. Father Christmas should be grateful because, although our house had a chimney, when we had tried lighting a fire the smoke filled the room and the fire went out. For Christmas Eve we all sat on the sofa in front of the empty grate, carefully laying the stockings round the chairs to ensure everyone would have a seat in the morning next to their surprise gifts.

"We mustn't forget to leave a drink out for Santa," I said.

"Orange juice?" asked Matthew.

"I was thinking he might like a whisky," Stephen suggested.

"What's whisky?" Matthew asked, cocking his head to one side.

Stephen looked as if he was about to explain the mechanics of fermentation and the benefits to the Scottish economy, but then thought better of it, settling for: "It's a drink for grown-ups."

I laughed. "You won't get away with that in ten years' time!"

"You're probably right. Come on, Matthew, you get a small glass out and I'll find the whisky."

While we waited for the boys, Eleanor wandered around the room straightening the stockings, and then climbed up next to me on the sofa. Thumb in mouth, she curled up under my arm.

"You OK?" I asked.

She nodded. The excitement of Christmas was exhausting and she was ready for bed.

"There we go!" declared Matthew, marching back into the room and carefully placing the whisky on the hearth. Stephen added a mince pie. Mustard raised his head for a look and took a big sniff.

"Ah, no you don't!" I shouted at him, as he stretched his legs and got up, inquisitively. Stephen grabbed him by the collar and took him out to the utility room.

Confused, Matthew asked, "Is Mustard OK?"

"Yes, he's fine, but we don't want him eating Father Christmas's treats, do we?"

Matthew looked horrified at the idea and repositioned the drink and mince pie.

"Do we need something for his reindeer?" I asked, thinking that we had some carrots in the fridge.

"I'll go!" Matthew jumped up and rushed through to the kitchen.

"Does he know where the carrots are?" I said in a low voice to Stephen.

"I wouldn't have thought so!" he whispered back, then in a louder voice, "Matthew! Do you need any help?"

There was the scraping of a chair by the breakfast bar (nowhere near the fridge) and then a satisfied, "Got it!" before he reappeared.

Carrying a banana.

He was surprised by our astonished faces. Accompanied by a patronising nodding of the head, he stated, as if explaining to a very slow child, "It's for the reindeer. For Santa's reindeer."

"Of course," I said, turning my open mouth into a beaming smile. "Of course. In Africa a reindeer would eat bananas."

And so the banana sat beside the whisky and the mince pie, waiting for our Father Christmas to come.

And come he did. The children were delighted by his visit, rushing to tell us about the pile of presents as the sun was still rising. Father Christmas himself wasn't interested in the banana, to be honest, but let's keep that secret to ourselves.

By lunchtime, Stephen was on the patio tending to the braai. He detested the job, but everyone knows it is the man's job to stand over the coals and the woman's to prepare salads in the kitchen. Who were we to break with tradition? He manfully prodded the chicken legs with a long-handled fork, hoping he'd know when they were properly cooked. I was either in the kitchen preparing our banquet (boiled potatoes and a salad) or walking from it to the table outside where we would eat. The children were happily ensconced in their bedroom playing with their new toys.

The braai was a total extravagance. We had probably burnt a measurable hole in the ozone layer for the sake of four measly-looking chicken legs. We might get some baked bananas out of the embers as well, but the size of the braai was disproportionate to the amount of food, and neither of us expected the children to eat much anyway. Despite our efforts, it was a most ordinary-looking Christmas dinner.

Stephen wandered into the garden occasionally to weed around the petunias and the marigolds, quickly returning to the shade of the patio to avoid the blistering sun. It was my third Christmas in the southern hemisphere and it still felt wrong to be celebrating in such heat. With luck it would cloud over by the end of the day and, with even more luck, rain overnight. However, at midday the sun was burning through a clear blue sky and the day was getting hotter. The covering over the terrace did a great job shading us from the sun's rays and kept the place relatively cool, which was why we always congregated under it. The braai's heat negated that effect.

"Church was good this morning," I said to Stephen, when we had a moment or two outside at the same time.

He grunted, and turned a chicken leg over. "You had the best position," he said.

"In what way?" I asked incredulously. "I was playing the piano!"

"Yes," he answered, not turning his head. "Playing meant you were at the front of church with a bit of space around you – enough space to move your arms and stuff to the music, whereas we barely had room to breathe!"

It had been crowded that morning, a hundred or more people crammed into the small room, but a wonderful atmosphere as we had celebrated the birth of Christ. We had sung just about every Christmas carol we could have thought of, although not (you wouldn't be surprised to hear) *See amid the winter's snow.*

"How close to being ready do you think we are?"

Stephen prodded at the chicken legs again. "Another five minutes?" he said questioningly.

"Great! Everything else is ready. I'll open a bottle of

wine."

"Fantastic. Although it might lengthen the cooking time." Stephen winked.

"I'll risk it!"

We clinked our glasses in celebration of the day. I sipped my wine, enjoying the contrast with the chaos of a couple of weeks earlier when we'd celebrated Matthew's birthday. Twenty children had come – nearly the whole class and a few add-on siblings. To my mind this had been madness in itself, as I worried about the amount of food I'd have to prepare. Sherry had a lot of merits, and was not inept at making food, but the majority of the burden had fallen to me, both in the planning and execution.

I had also been anxious that it might rain, as it had been particularly wet in early December. If it had done, I would have had to have brought all the children inside. It was a big house, but twenty hyper children in my living room for two hours brought out my claustrophobic instincts. From experience I knew that their parents, for the most part, took the birthday party as an opportunity to do Christmas shopping. I had been left with Stephen – still easily exhausted as a result of his Brain Event – as my main source of support.

I need not have worried. He had planned game after game, enjoying every minute of the party. The children had chewed on fizzy sweets hung from the ceiling. They had flapped paper fish across the living room floor. Best of all, they had done a treasure hunt around the garden, which involved a lot of running (tiring them out) and a few questions (perplexing them). Poor old Mustard had been bamboozled by the entire event and was none too chuffed at being locked away in the utility room for the afternoon.

Success had been measured by Matthew's reaction, who had decided that he ought to have parties more often and had booked his next one in for August, on his father's birthday. In the tranquillity of Christmas Day, I wondered if we'd still be here.

"Isn't it funny," I said to Stephen, "that I proposed an extra year here, and we're halfway through that already, and you haven't even begun your time back in the UK."

"I haven't begun writing up the PhD yet," he warned me. "It's going to take a long time."

I dismissed that instantly. *It's just a few thousand words – it can't take too long to type. And besides, if he's on his own in the UK he'll have plenty of time for that.*

Still, it was ironic that eighteen months after Margriet and Jenny had told me to stay an extra year, we were doing just that, through no action of my own. Stephen's research had demanded an extra six months, then his Brain Event had resulted in a second six-month extension. The original two-year placement had now become three years. I was getting my wish to stay in Zambia without (yet) losing my husband. The tricky decisions were still to come, but I'd made it through a difficult year and still felt confident. In this golden moment of peace on Christmas Day – children self-entertained, and a glass of wine in hand – I was totally comfortable with our intentions. If nothing else, the last year had taught me that I could not plan too far ahead: life had a habit of leaping in and messing the situation up.

"I think they're done," Stephen said, turning the chicken over one last time.

"OK – you get the children, I'll bring the rest of the food out," I said, reluctantly putting down my wine glass and returning to the kitchen.

"Lunch is ready!" Stephen called through the children's bedroom window. "Go wash your hands and then come outside."

There was a flurry of activity and door-slamming as they dropped their toys at the promise of food. I hurried around with plates and food, arranging us all around the plastic garden table. I smiled at Matthew and Eleanor's eager faces, blonde-haired and sun-bronzed, thinking how blessed I was to have such a wonderful family. A chicken leg and some salads: welcome to an easy Christmas lunch.

❧

After lunch I completed the finishing touches to my own Christmas present. Stephen had organised the construction of a large wooden pillar, carefully treated against termites, which had been fixed in the ground a couple of metres from the avocado tree on the front lawn. A large notch was carved in one side just below eye-height. Secured with knotting at the tree end and a careful hooking of rope at the other, I was finally able to hang the hammock my sister had sent me for my birthday eight months earlier.

Matthew and Mustard had followed me across the lawn. Mustard sniffed around the foot of the pillar and then settled himself in the shade of the tree. Matthew was far more excited. He'd watched the post being cemented into the hole earlier in the week and was curious to know how it all hung together. Though he wasn't much help tying it up (boy scouts and knots were a few years away yet) he was a very willing guinea pig.

"Want a go, Matthew?"

"Yes please!"

He ran over and tried to heave himself up, but it was set at an adult height.

"Here, I'll lift you," I said. I placed him in the hammock, where he lay still for approximately two seconds before fidgeting and wanting to get out.

"You're supposed to lie there and relax!" I said, and further rhapsodised: "Allow the cares of the world to disappear, forget all your troubles, even doze, not– whoa!"

I caught him before he fell out. My fantasy was of no interest to him, particularly not when he had plenty of new gifts waiting elsewhere.

"Going to see Daddy!" he said, and ran inside. There was no keeping him still, even though I was aware Daddy was doing the washing-up – an even less exciting prospect.

"Looks like its just you and me, Mustard," I said, bending down to pat him on the head. His ears lifted in appreciation, but the torpor of a hot, humid afternoon wasn't moving him from the shadow of the tree.

I turned back to look at my hammock. It was high, but I could sit on it… swing my legs round and…

I lay back and enjoyed the dappled sunlight dancing through the leaves of the avocado tree. I could see a couple of fruit filling out with the gift of the rainy season. The tree was hardly heavy-laden, and wasn't likely to produce anywhere near as much as the other avocado tree near the vegetable plot at the back.

Yes, I thought, rocking gently, *I could get used to this.*

I closed my eyes. *What a way to spend Christmas!* It was nearly a year since I had lain in that bed in Nsobe, not sleeping because of Eleanor and planning the year ahead. *Just think what I've achieved!* We'd moved house; the family had increased by a dog, two cats and eight fish; I'd travelled to the DRC; I'd coped with termites in the kitchen and a water shortage on the plot; I'd camped in the bush in Africa; I'd caught a tiger fish.

And that was just Zambia. The Brain Event had brought a whole new level of fear and anxiety into my life. Adding in the worries about Eleanor's hearing and the grommet operation, I had spent more time in hospitals in the last three months than I would ever ask for. It was noticeable that Eleanor could now hear better and (when she chose to) obeyed instructions that I shouted to her. The need for her to watch my lips, or touch my face, had gone. Her verbal skills would take longer to materialise but, for now, everyone seemed pleased with her progress.

Stephen's health was improving daily. His six-week check-up had revealed little other than to confirm he would be better off with an insulin pump rather than injections. They weren't prepared to provide him with one unless they could monitor him regularly, which meant him being resident in the UK. His proposed return for a year would satisfy that requirement and, though that left us a difficult eight months ahead, it felt manageable. The prognosis was good.

And to think: just three months earlier I'd worried whether he'd ever communicate properly again: talk in full sentences, retrieve words, cope with the efforts of social interaction. He had finally completed one of the concise crosswords all by himself. It was such an achievement he celebrated with a Mosi. He had been avoiding alcohol since The Brain Event as it made controlling his blood sugars more difficult. However, some events simply require celebrations, and he enjoyed the drink enormously. He couldn't complete the crossword the next day though…

His workload had gradually been increasing – mornings that had lengthened to beyond lunch and even a couple of pretty full days. He hoped to manage a full week of short days in January and to be full time again by Easter. Easter would also bring Gwyn and Gareth's wedding, and I was delighted my fears over Stephen not being able to cope with such an event had all but disappeared.

We were all very excited about The Wedding, except Matthew who didn't want to wear the shirt I'd bought for him because it had buttons on it. Gwyn and Gareth were planning to get married on the plot out of town where – eventually – they'd build their new home. A small army of people were clearing the bush and planting grass that would hopefully root well in the rains. I hoped the men they employed were better at watering than mine.

I chastised myself. *They aren't too bad.* I was fortunate to have reliable staff, and I noticed their absence on Christmas Day. It all felt very subdued, with none of the hurly-burly I remembered of Christmases growing up. Other than church, we had been just the four of us, as Gwyn chose to spend the day with Gareth's family and the rest of our blood relations were thousands of miles away.

"Thought you'd like this!"

I nearly fell out of the hammock at the shock of hearing Stephen's voice. He was standing with a replenished glass of wine in his hand.

"Thank you," I said when I recovered my poise. "That's lovely."

"Is the hammock OK?" he asked, checking out the structure and knots.

I swung my legs round. "It's lovely. Want to join me? I'll need to sit up to hold that drink anyway."

We sat side by side, swinging companionably as we looked out over the garden, now a fresh green as the rains had taken hold. The mud runways that the pipework trenches had created were vanishing as the grass regrew. *The healing power of nature, visible on my lawn and working on my husband and daughter,* I thought.

There was a crack overhead, followed by a thud on the ground. Mustard's ears pricked, he stood up, stretched and went over to investigate. He took the fallen avocado to a safe distance and began chewing the solid fruit.

"Glad to have dodged that bullet," Stephen said.

"We've dodged a few this year, haven't we," I replied. I peered up through the leaves and branches. I couldn't see any above us.

"Seems you don't get rid of me that easily," he said.

I grinned at Stephen and settled back to enjoy my drink. Like the last year, whatever had been thrown at us, we'd survived. I had more than I could ever want: a lovely home, family and friends around me, even a wedding to look forward to. Our roots in Zambia were more and more established.

I lay back and shut my eyes. "Everything's just perfect," I whispered to the leaves in the tree. "Perfect."

BEWARE THE FALLING AVOCADOS

Beware the falling avocados.
Your Daddy does and your Mama does.
Even your Just Grandpapa does,
     Therefore you should do so too.

Where this notice is displayed-o
It should always be obeyed-o
Wise men shun the avocado
     So should girls and boys like you.

It amounts to sheer bravado
To rest beneath an avocado,
Especially in a tornado,
     But even in a gentle breeze.

For its fruit is big and hard-o
And it could catch you off your guard-o
So avoid the avocado:
     Shelter under other trees.

For Matthew & Eleanor, from Just Grandpa
(c) J M Sharman, April 2005

*Inspired by a notice on the large avocado tree outside the café in
the Agricultural Showgrounds, Lusaka.
This tree has subsequently been chopped down.*

ABOUT THE AUTHOR

Born and brought up in Yorkshire, educated in Scotland, Catharine also lived in Cambridge and London before moving to Lusaka, Zambia. She is a fully qualified chartered accountant, married with two children and currently lives near Manchester. In her spare time she enjoys playing the cello, watching cricket, preaching and winning at board games, but not all at once.

Her first volume of memoir, *In the Shade of the Mulberry Tree*, was shortlisted for the Self-Publishing Book of the Year Award 2014.

DIABETES

Diabetes mellitus is a condition where blood sugar levels are too high. Normally, the hormone insulin controls blood sugar levels by enabling glucose to enter the body's cells to be used as energy.

Type 1 diabetes, where the body doesn't make insulin, which Stephen has, usually develops before the age of 40 and has to be treated with regular injections of insulin. Type 2 diabetes, where there is not enough insulin or the body is resistant to insulin, is more common in the elderly and can often be treated by tablets or, if mild, diet alone.

Before meeting Stephen I had negligible knowledge of diabetes. My mother-in-law encouraged me to read 'Balance', the magazine from Diabetes UK, just so I would have a better idea of how to look after her son. As you can tell, I haven't always got it right.

Nevertheless, I can thoroughly recommend the resources of Diabetes UK (www.diabetes.org.uk), who have a seemingly infinite amount of support for people suffering from Type 1 or Type 2 Diabetes and their families and carers. The website also has links if you would like to support their work to prevent and, one day, cure the condition.

RECOMMENDED READING:

In the Footsteps of Mr Kurtz: Living on the Brink of Disaster in the Congo, Michaela Wrong, published by Fourth Estate.

Catharine
Withenay

IN THE SHADE OF THE
MULBERRY
TREE

A year in Zambia

Organising her husband, toddler and babe in arms, three suitcases, two rucksacks, a pram and a travel cot onto a plane ready for a new life in Zambia is complicated enough. Given Catharine's fear of malaria and tropical diseases and the anxieties of moving beyond the reach of friends and family, she wonders how she was persuaded to move at all. Then, just as they approach the airport, it appears that they don't have their passports.

In the Shade of the Mulberry Tree is a heartwarming and thought provoking tale about Catharine Withenay's first year living abroad as an expatriate wife. She chronicles her family's adventures as they settle into a new culture far from home. Nothing is as simple as it should be, from buying furniture to getting a haircut. As she copes with motherhood and the injustices of poverty and healthcare in Zambia she wonders: could she ever come to call this place home?

Catharine Withenay

Follow Catharine on Twitter
@c_withenay

Made in the USA
Charleston, SC
17 May 2016